THE AEROSPACE HERITAGE
OF LONG ISLAND

LONG ISLAND STUDIES

THE AEROSPACE HERITAGE
OF LONG ISLAND

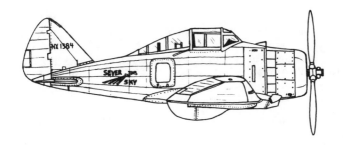

by
Joshua Stoff

Heart of the Lakes Publishing
Interlaken, New York
1989

Copyright © 1989
Long Island Studies Institute
Hofstra University, Hempstead, NY 11550
All rights reserved

Cover illustration by Joshua Stoff. Photographs not otherwise credited are from the collections of the Nassau County Museum.

Library of Congress Cataloging-in-Publication Data

Stoff, Joshua.
    Aerospace heritage of Long Island / by Joshua Stoff.

    (Long Island studies)
    Includes bibliographical references.
    Includes index.
    1. Aerospace industries—New York (State)—Long Island—
History.   2. Aircraft Industry—New York (State)—Long Island—
History.   3. Aeronautics—New York   (State)—Long   Island—
History.   I. Title.   II. Series.

HD9711.5.U62L62   1989   /0.00 PB   89-39400
338.4'76291'0974721—dc20   CIP
ISBN: 1-55787-056-X (pbk.)

Manufactured in the United States of America

A *quality* publication of
Heart of the Lakes Publishing
Interlaken, New York 14847

Contents

Charles Lindbergh in his Ryan NYP *Spirit of St. Louis* over Roosevelt Field, May 20, 1927.

Foreword

Many Americans are familiar with Wilbur and Orville Wright's historic first sustained flight of a power-driven airplane at Kill Devil Hill near Kitty Hawk on the Outer Banks of North Carolina. But if North Carolina's license plates rightly declare it "First in Flight," surely Long Island nurtured aviation in its infancy and well deserves the designation of the "Cradle of Aviation." Indeed, Nassau County has been developing a major air-space museum dedicated to this aspect of its history.

Many "firsts" in aviation occurred on Long Island. Long before Charles Lindbergh's famous solo flight from Roosevelt Field across the Atlantic in 1927, other men and women had made pioneering flights from Long Island in aviation's "Golden Age." Long Island's proximity to New York City and its natural terrain made it an ideal site for airfields, many of which were located on the Hempstead Plains in central Nassau County. Moreover, Long Island has been home to many airplane and aerospace companies. Sperry and Curtiss, which began during World War I, and Republic and Grumman, which began in the 1930s, were among the larger and better known of the companies, but more than 20 others produced aircraft on Long Island.

Long Island firms have had an important role in spaceflight. Grumman produced the historic Lunar Module which landed on the moon in 1969. In the 1980s Grumman was the largest private employer in Nassau and Suffolk counties and many other companies were involved in subcontracts producing components for the aerospace industry.

Long Island's aviation history has not been easily accessible to general readers. Histories of Long Island mention it briefly, and more specialized works go into greater detail on specific aspects. Hofstra's 1968 Yearbook of Business edited by William K. Kaiser provided a useful initial overview of Long Island's aerospace industry for the years 1904–1964. (After Kaiser left Hofstra, he was associated with Nassau County's aviation museum.) When

8

the Long Island Studies Institute began a series of Long Island Studies publications, we requested Joshua Stoff, Curator of the Cradle of Aviation Museum at Mitchel Field to prepare this work. Mr. Stoff has written articles and books on various aspects of Long Island's aerospace heritage, including the making of the Lunar Module, Roosevelt Field Airport, and Republic Aviation Corporation.

This book focuses on geographical Long Island and hence includes flights, airfields, and companies in Brooklyn and Queens as well as Nassau and Suffolk counties. Long Island's extensive involvement in aerospace is an important part of the island's twentieth century history. It is a proud heritage making Long Island worthy of being called the "Cradle of Aviation."

Natalie A. Naylor, Director
Long Island Studies Institute

Introduction

In less than 80 years, aviation has grown, boomed, and declined on Long Island. Long Island has helped transform aviation from a dangerous sport to a viable means of commercial transportation. It has also produced a large portion of the nation's aerial arsenal in time of war. The many record-setting and historic flights that transpired here, and the many aviation companies that developed here made aviation the integral part of our world that it is today. This is a brief survey of Long Island's involvement in, and contribution to, the history of aviation and spaceflight.

Long Island was geographically a natural airfield. The Island itself is ideally placed at the eastern edge of the United States, at the western edge of the Atlantic Ocean, and adjacent to America's most populous city. This made it the ideal focal point for most transatlantic and transcontinental flights. Furthermore, the central area of Nassau County, known as the Hempstead Plains, was the only natural prairie east of the Allegheny Mountains. This proved to be an ideal flying field, treeless and flat, with only tall grasses and scattered farmhouses. The Hempstead Plains was to be the scene of intense aviation activity for over 50 years.

The contributions by many Long Islanders and Long Island corporations to the subsequent technical development of aviation and spaceflight, and their key roles in making aviation central to our world today will be made clear. Although this work is obviously a brief one, it is intended to give some insight into, and understanding of, the important aeronautical activity that has taken place on Long Island in the twentieth century. To date no detailed work of any sort has attempted to cover the aerospace heritage of Long Island and present it in one volume for the student, researcher, scholar, and general public. Some of the more technical information on aircraft production by the various companies has been included in an appendix.

Nassau County has undertaken the development of a major Air and Space Museum because of the vast amount of historic aerospace activity that has taken place on Long Island. This museum , known as the Cradle of Aviation Museum and located at Mitchel Field, Garden City, has as its primary mission to gather, preserve, and interpret the aerospace heritage of Long Island. Some 40 historic aircraft and spacecraft have been procured, most of them built on Long Island and each directly relevant to our aerospace heritage. These aircraft have been obtained by private and corporate donation, governmental loan, or purchase by the museum's support organization, the Friends for Long Island's Heritage. The vast majority have been painstakingly and accurately restored by the museum's skilled volunteer corps. To date, the Museum has been located in two deteriorating hangars on historic Mitchel Field. The county plans a major renovation and expansion of these structures. Private fundraising plays a key role in this project. When completed, the Cradle of Aviation Museum will be a world-class museum, clearly befitting our extensive aerospace heritage.

The first aircraft to fly over Long Island
was a Lilienthal Glider in1896

The Dawn of Flight

From the very dawn of human flight Long Island has been intimately tied to the history of aeronautics and has helped define the direction it was to take. The earliest form of flight by man was ballooning, and this nascent form of travel made its presence known on Long Island. However, ballooning never became popular on Long Island due to its being a relatively small body of land surrounded by water. Early balloonists had no desire to get blown out to sea! Nonetheless, in June 1833 Charles Durant lifted off from the Manhattan Battery and landed in Jamaica, thus becoming the first man to set foot on Long Island coming from the skies. In 1866, Solomon Andrews flew in a cigar-shaped balloon from New York City to Astoria. However, the greatest balloon flight from Long Island occurred in 1873. W.H. Donaldson, with the help of noted American balloonist John Wise, built a huge balloon called the *Daily Graphic,* named after the newspaper that funded its construction. Donaldson planned on attempting the first crossing of the Atlantic Ocean by air. After test flights were made in September, the transatlantic flight took off from Brooklyn on October 7. Unfortunately, their daring venture did not last very long. The balloon encountered a violent storm over Connecticut forcing the three-man crew to jump out to safety. Thus, the first attempted transatlantic flight from Long Island lasted only 60 miles. But there would be more. In July 1874, in another balloon, Donaldson flew from New York City to Hempstead, the first aerial voyage to terminate in what is now Nassau County. Subsequently, there were sporadic balloon ascents made on Long Island, some even as late as the early 1900s.[1] However, the key to flight by man clearly lay in winged, powered flight. Here too, Long Island played a key role.

In the 1860s, an English minister named Charles Edwards emigrated to Greenwich Point (later Roosevelt). He was deeply interested in aeronautical experimentation, and through the 1870s he built gliders with bamboo frames in his barn/workshop.

Purportedly, his son flew one from a local water tower. Edwards also built scale flying bamboo models of his designs and even planned on incorporating steam engines for powered flights in larger craft. For unknown reasons though, Edwards discontinued his experimentation in the late 1870s.[2]

The first documented aircraft flight on Long Island occurred in 1896. William Randolph Hearst apparently wanting to create headlines for his newspaper, the *New York Journal*, purchased a German Lilienthal hang glider. There appear to have been several successful flights made on a friend's Long Island estate, possibly at Sands Point, by Harry Bodine. Fortunately, this oldest surviving aircraft to have flown on Long Island still exists and is now on display at the National Air & Space Museum in Washington, D.C.[3]

The first successful powered flights in the United States also occurred on Long Island, even prior to the Wright Brothers. However, these lighter-than-air flights were not made in airplanes. In 1902, two small dirigibles soared over Brighton Beach, Brooklyn. Leo Stevens, in an airship of his own design, and

Leo Stevens' airship in flight over Brooklyn, 1902.

Edward Boyce in the rebuilt Santos-Dumont airship Number 6, both took to the air on September 30. Equipped with engines of about 10 horsepower, each navigated the skies for flights of about 45 minutes. However, both soon made forced landings due to mechanical problems. Although they had little impact on the subsequent development of aviation, powered flight had come to Long Island to stay.[4]

At about the turn of the century, inventors around the world began to experiment with powered heavier-than-air flight as recent advances in engines and aerodynamic theory made such an idea feasible for the first time. Long Island was no exception. Two little-known Long Islanders of this early flight period should be noted. They are Charles Manly and Augustus Herring, both Freeport residents. Manly was the assistant, engineer, and pilot for Dr. Samuel Langley at the turn of the century. Langley was funded by the U.S. War Department in his efforts to build a man-carrying aircraft. For this tandem wing aircraft, or "Aerodrome," Manly built an advanced 52 horsepower rotary engine in Washington, D.C. This engine was far superior to that used by the Wright brothers. Although in 1903 two unsuccessful attempts were made to launch Langley's aircraft from a houseboat on the Potomac, with Manly as pilot, Manly's one-fourth scale steam-powered model of the Langley Aerodrome flew well. The 1902 Langley is generally acknowledged as being the first aircraft "capable" of powered flight. However, on December 17, 1903, the Wright brothers achieved the world's first sustained, controlled powered flight, when their Wright Flyer soared over the dunes of Kitty Hawk, North Carolina.

Augustus Herring was one of the earliest American experimenters with gliders and powered aircraft. In the 1880s, he built gliders of his own design and in 1893 he purchased a Lilienthal hang glider which he flew in the west Bronx. By 1894 Herring had built steam-powered model aircraft that successfully flew which proved that mechanical flight was possible. Herring went to Chicago in 1896 and worked with gliding pioneer Octave Chanute as a member of his team for gliding experiments in Michigan. Herring developed biplane (two wings) and triplane (three wings) gliders in 1896 with movable "regulator" tails in order to help achieve stability. A powered version of the triplane was patented in England, but the U.S. patent was rejected as the

Patent Office believed powered flight was an undemonstrated theory. However, while in Michigan in 1898, Herring built and flew a powered biplane of his own design which ran on a compressed air engine. The plane was flown twice in Michigan with Herring as pilot for about ten seconds each time.

Herring never claimed that he was the first "to fly," but he did prove the problem of powered flight solvable when he achieved an airborne condition. Nonetheless, this was not sustained, controlled flight. Herring worked with Langley in 1900 and persuaded him to use cambered (curved) wings on his "aerodrome" instead of flat ones. In 1908, in New York City, Herring built an unsuccessful frail twin engine biplane for the Army Aircraft competition won by the Wrights in Fort Meyer, Virginia.

Herring purportedly attempted to fly and crashed this aircraft in Freeport. But in 1909, he raised the money needed to help put Glenn Curtiss into the business of manufacturing aircraft. Thus the 1909 Herring-Curtiss *Golden Flyer* incorporated ideas of both experimenters, and it was this aircraft that later flew in Mineola in 1909. Herring's house, at 309 South Main Street, Freeport, still stands.[5]

The first powered aircraft flights on Long Island occurred in August 1908, although they were somewhat of a debacle. Pioneer French aviator Henri Farman brought his Voisin biplane to New York for a series of public flights from the Brighton Beach Racetrack. Over the course of a week, when there was no wind, Farman made short flights for the small, paying crowd in attendance. These flights were only about 10 feet high and about 500 yards long—in a straight line—not really sustained, controlled flight. Farman considered the exhibition a failure due to the performance of the machine, and the little interest it attracted.[6]

Wings Over the Hempstead Plains

In 1909 the first tentative flights were made from the central area of Nassau County, then known as the Hempstead Plains. This inaugurated aviation to an area where it was to remain the focus of intense aeronautical activity for the next 50 years. During 1909, the Aeronautic Society of New York ordered a pusher biplane from Glenn Curtiss of Hammondsport, New York. It was the first commercial sale of an aircraft in the United States. This aircraft, the *Golden Flyer*, was delivered to Morris Park racetrack in the Bronx, where it made a few short flights. Unhappy with the cramped surroundings, Curtiss looked for a more acceptable area to fully test his new creation. A day trip to Long Island revealed Mineola to be "a nice flat place," so Curtiss and the Aeronautic Society moved their equipment and activity here.

They set up camp in Mineola, just east of the Fairgrounds (now the site of the Nassau County court houses). By July, Curtiss made his first real flights in the *Golden Flyer* and he expressed his happiness both with his machine and his new surroundings. He was so pleased, in fact, that he decided to make an attempt at the Scientific American Trophy for the first flight of 25 kilometers. Thus on the still morning of July 17, 1909, at 5:16 a.m., Curtiss took off from Mineola and successfully circled the field for 30 minutes at treetop height. Curtiss had won the $10,000 prize for the longest flight (16 miles) by an American to date. Aviation was on its way. Later that summer Curtiss made the first "cross-country" flight from Mineola. He flew east toward Meadow Brook (roughly where the parkway is now), banked over Westbury, and returned to Mineola flying 28 miles in 58 minutes. Curtiss really taught himself to fly on Long Island. He learned how to successfully takeoff and land and how to make graceful circles. He trained on the Hempstead Plains for the upcoming Rheims Aviation Meet in France, where he set a world speed record. Curtiss also taught a pupil, Charles Willard, who thus became the first man to learn to fly on Long Island. By the end of 1909, the

The Herring-Curtiss *Golden Flyer*, 1909.

Aeronautic Society put up its first building on its airfield on Washington Avenue, Garden City. This hangar soon housed seven aircraft. There were also numerous white tents and other "flying machines" on exhibit. Most of the flying was done in the early morning or late afternoon when the winds were least. Soon Long Islanders came to the field in droves on nice days to see the miracle of human flight.[1]

By October 1909, Frank Van Anden of Islip built and flew a biplane of his own design from the Mineola flying field. It was but the first of thousands of aircraft eventually to be built on Long Island. Also in October, Wilbur Wright made the most daring flight on Long Island to date, when he flew his Wright biplane from Garden City to Manhattan and back.

In December 1909, the first American designed and built monoplane also made its debut on Long Island, when Dr. Henry Walden flew his Walden III at Mineola. Powered by a three-cylinder Anzani engine, the diminutive monoplane reached speeds of 50 mph. The Walden III was preceded by two tandem biplanes, one of which flew briefly as early as 1907. In all, Walden built 12 aircraft over a four-year period. His most successful design was the Walden IX in which he competed in air meets in Boston, Brighton Beach, and St. Louis in 1911.[2]

In 1909 the Aero Club of Long Island was established.

Although it only contained 13 members it remained in loose operation until 1913. The Aero Club was organized by the Newell brothers who built and flew a small glider in Richmond Hill in 1909 and 1910. Fellow member Tom Kramer also flew a glider towed behind a car, in Oceanside in 1909. The most successful member was Charles Wald who briefly operated an Air Ferry from Glenwood Landing to New Rochelle in a Wright-type aircraft in 1912.[3]

Among the many pioneer aircraft inventors working on Long Island were Albert and Arthur Heinrich of Baldwin. Starting in 1910, they built some of the earliest and fastest American monoplanes. Working in their barn/factory in Baldwin, they produced the Model A, the first American monoplane powered by an American engine. The Model A was also among the first aircraft to incorporate the modern aileron (control surface used for banking) design. The Heinrich brothers taught themselves to fly on this aircraft and by 1912 they had opened their own flying school at the Hempstead Plains Aerodrome. Heinrich produced several monoplane and biplane designs including the rotary-engine biplane Heinrich *Victor*, built for the Air Corps in World War I.[4] The company ceased operation in 1918.

The year 1910 was a remarkable one for American aviation, and it was led by developments taking place on Long Island. In August, Clifford Harmon made a dangerous long-distance flight, when he flew his Farman biplane across Long Island Sound from Mineola to Greenwich, Connecticut. On August 4, Elmo Pickerill purportedly made the first wireless (radio) transmission from an aircraft. He flew his Wright Model B from Mineola to Manhattan Beach and there contacted several ground stations. Also in August, an Aerial Exhibition was held at the racetrack in Sheepshead Bay, Brooklyn. The most important development at this meet was when the future military potential of the aircraft was demonstrated. Flying with Glenn Curtiss, Army Lieutenant J. Fickel fired several rifle shots at targets on the ground. It was a portent of things to come.

On September 26, 1910, Bessica Raiche took off from the Hempstead Plains and thus became the first American woman to pilot an airplane. Although the pioneering flight ended in a crash, Raiche remained undeterred and along with her husband, she built a pusher biplane at her home in Mineola.

By far the biggest aeronautical event on Long Island to date was the 1910 International Aviation Meet at Belmont Park. Running from October 22–31, it was the largest international air meet in the United States up to this time. The greatest aviators from all over America and Europe came to Long Island to exhibit their newest machines, race, set records, and win prize money. The huge air meet at Belmont Park Racetrack was front-page news across America all through the week. The spectacle drew large crowds as most people had never seen an aircraft and they personally wanted to witness this new wonder of flight. The Wright brothers and Glenn Curtiss were in attendance as well as the best-known European aviators. There were daily altitude contests, distance runs, speed races, and cross-country races with prizes totaling $75,000—a considerable sum for 1910. Flying Wright biplanes, Wright company pilots Arch Hoxsey and Ralph Johnstone fought for the altitude prize as they flew their frail wood and wire aircraft literally out of sight. Johnstone set a new world's altitude record—a remarkable 9,714 feet. The previous record set in Rheims was approximately 500 feet. Aviation was truly making remarkable advances. The biggest events of the meet were the Gordon Bennett and Statue of Liberty races. The Gordon Bennett 100 kilometer speed race was won by England's Claude Grahame-White, flying 61 mph in a Bleriot. The Statue of Liberty race drew over 75,000 spectators to see a spectacular race from Belmont Park around the Statue of Liberty and back. This was a long, dangerous flight for 1910, flying over open water and congested cities. Americans desperately wanted an American to win the race around this national symbol. Fortunately, American John Moisant, in a just-purchased Bleriot narrowly won the race, beating Claude Grahame-White by 43 seconds. He immediately became a national hero. The Belmont Park Meet not only helped foster the technical development of aviation, it also focused public attention on it, thereby increasing its support and popularity.[5]

By 1911, the Mineola airfield was found to be too small and congested. Thus most flying moved to the new Hempstead Plains Aerodrome, east of Clinton Road, Garden City. It was this field that was eventually to become the world reknowned Roosevelt Field. The Hempstead Plains Field was much larger and more open than the old airfield. By the summer of 1911, consisting of nearly 1,000 acres housing some 25 wooden hangars, grandstands, and pylons, it was called the finest flying field in the United States. In the spring of 1911 the Moisant School opened here, founded by Alfred Moisant, John's brother. This was the first civilian flying school in America. The Moisant School had five of its own hangars and seven Bleriot monoplanes. They ran a five-week flying course for $750. The Moisant School gave instruction based on the mechanical knowledge of the aircraft, as well as flight and classroom instruction. This school was also very unusual in that it welcomed women (the Wright and Curtiss schools did not). Thus the first licensed American woman pilot, Harriet Quimby, was trained at the Moisant School. Soloing in August 1911, she later became the first woman to fly the English Channel. America's second licensed woman pilot, Matilde Moisant, also learned here.[6] In fact many of the earliest American fliers were trained on Long Island. By 1912, the Aero Club of America (not related to the Aero Club of Long Island) moved to the Hempstead Plains Field. Another aeronautical pioneer, Giuseppe Bellanca, operated his own flying school on the field and built his first aircraft here. The first all-metal (structure only) monoplane in America, built by Walter Fairchild, was also constructed on the Hempstead Plains Field in 1912.

In the summer of 1911, the American Aeroplane Supply House (AASH) opened in Hempstead. This was the first of many aircraft manufacturing companies to operate on Long Island. The AASH basically built and sold copies of French Bleriot-type monoplanes. In fact, one currently owned by Cole Palen of Old Rhinebeck Aerodrome is the oldest surviving Long Island built aircraft. Between 1911 and 1913, four basic models were produced, costing between $2,700 and $6,000 depending on the type of engine. These included racing and military models (two seats). During 1911, AASH sold more Bleriots than all other U.S. manufacturers combined. However, in all they only produced about 15 aircraft and ceased operation in 1914.[7]

On September 17, 1911, a most daring aeronautical adventure began on Long Island. Cal Rodgers in a Wright EX biplane named the *Vin Fiz*, took off from Sheepshead Bay, Brooklyn, and flew to California in 49 days, with 11 crashes along the way. Due to the limitations of aircraft at the time, Rodgers could only fly during daylight and in good weather. Rodgers was attempting to win the $50,000 Hearst prize for the first flight

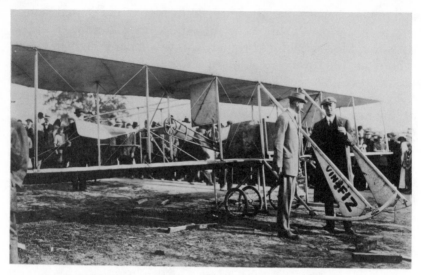

Cal Rodgers and the Wright EX *Vin Fiz*, 1911.

across America within 30 days. Rodgers took too long to win the prize, but he wanted to finish just to prove it could be done. A train followed him the entire journey, carrying enough spare parts to keep rebuilding his plane after every mishap. As there were no airfields in most of the country at that time, every landing in an unfamiliar field was a dangerous one. Nonetheless this first transcontinental air trip showed the future potential of the airplane.[8]

In October 1911 a Second International Air Meet was held on Long Island, this time at the Nassau Boulevard Airfield in Garden City. This field, which was lined with 20 small wooden hangars, drew many aviators and aircraft for the meet. The most interesting, if not the most important, event of the meet was the first official airmail flight in the United States. Postmaster General Frank Hitchcock set up a temporary post office on the field and pilot Earle Ovington made daily airmail flights to Mineola in his Bleriot. Ovington, designated U.S. Mail Pilot #1, flew with the mail bags on his lap and dropped them over Mineola. Although it was only a six-mile airmail flight, airmail was here to stay.[9] Nassau Boulevard was also the site of the first official appearance of Army fliers at an air meet. Two Army aviators flying Burgess-Wright machines demonstrated the reconnaissance potential of the airplane when they located soldiers concealed in nearby woods.

However, up until World War I, flying was still regarded as somewhat of a spectator sport. This was further evidenced on Long Island in 1912 and 1913 when Lincoln Beachy in a Curtiss-type pusher gave shows at the Brighton Beach Racetrack. Beachy raced Barney Oldfield in his car and did other dangerous acrobatics. However, the scientific development of aviation was also taking place on Long Island at the same time. In 1914, Lawrence Sperry won an important air safety prize in Paris for the development of an operational gyro-stabilizing device for an aircraft. The gyroscope, built by the Sperry Company in Brooklyn, stabilized a Curtiss Flying Boat in flight without pilot input. It was one of the first great steps in making flying safe.

Basic flight training brought with it many accidents; in 1918
this Jenny wound up in a Long Island potato field.

World War I—War in the Sky

When the U.S. entered World War I in 1917, the Hempstead Plains Airfield was one of only two Army flying fields in the country. It all began in July 1916 with the delivery of four Army Curtiss JN-4 "Jenny" trainers to the Hempstead Plains Airfield, Mineola. There, Lt. Joseph Carberry had officially opened the Army Aviation School at the Signal Corps Aviation Station-Mineola, on July 22. However there were still civilian flying operations on the field and the Army was left with a few old hangars and little staff. The New York National Guard First Aero Company began training on the field in 1915, thus becoming the first, and only, flying Guard unit in the country (three aircraft). The private Aero Club of America provided the financial support for the Guard. Carberry was assigned the task of examining fliers for assignment to squadron duty on the chaotic Mexican border; he could even hire civilians for this duty as the Army had so few fliers. Thus the first American aviators to see combat were trained on Long Island, as they later searched Mexico for Pancho Villa in 1916 and 1917. At the time, there was virtually no federal funding for army aviation. In 1916, the Aero Club of America purchased a Curtiss Twin JN with a recoilless cannon for the squadron on duty on the Mexican border. Sufficient funds were available to train only one officer from each state to fly![1]

In 1917, the Hempstead Plains Airfield was renamed Hazelhurst Field in honor of a deceased Army flier. At the end of 1916, Congress passed a massive federal appropriation for military aviation. Shortly thereafter, 12 new Jennies were sent to Mineola. As the Mexican Border quieted down, the role of the Mineola Field changed to that of a testing station, both because of its proximity to New York and the lack of an experimental field to test new flight equipment. Almost any item of equipment which could be carried on an aircraft seems to have been tried including instruments, cameras, signalling devices, flight apparel, propellers, bombs, bomb-dropping devices, automatic stabilization devices, and radios. Thus the frontiers of military aviation were being pushed back at Mineola. This emphasis on experimental work deterred training, but there were still some machines available for training New York Guard and civilian students. On November 18, the National Guard made its first "cross-country" flight when a formation of seven Jennies flew nonstop from Mineola to Princeton. Cross-country flights also continued through the winter in order to test new flight clothing. Thus the earliest military experience with winter flying was gained on Long Island.

All military personnel on the field lived in tents until 1917 when new barracks and a mess hall were built. By the end of 1917, the Army had 18 students at Mineola and the field began to expand rapidly as the U.S. became more fully engaged in World War I. In March 1917, Army ground forces made a simulated attack on Mineola. Twenty-five planes took off from Mineola to find "enemy forces." The group located artillery, motor supply columns, and troops in only 85 minutes. The Army clearly was experimenting with the newly developed art of aerial reconnaissance.

During 1917, one of the many Army fliers trained at Hazelhurst Field was Quentin Roosevelt, ex-President Theodore Roosevelt's son. Unfortunately, Quentin was killed in action while flying a Nieuport 28 in 1918. Hazelhurst Field was subsequently renamed for him in July 1918. Today a shopping mall still bears his name. In 1917, a new Army aviation field, Field #2, was established just south of Hazelhurst Field to serve as an additional training and storage base. Jennies became a common sight over Long Island in 1917 and 1918. Hundreds of aviators were trained for war at these training fields, two of the largest in the United States. Numerous new wooden buildings and tents were erected on Roosevelt and Field #2 in 1918 in order to meet this rapid expansion. In July 1918, Field #2 was renamed Mitchel Field in honor of former New York City Mayor John Purroy Mitchel who was killed while training for the Air Service in Louisiana. Additional Army flight training was conducted at Brindley Field in Commack.

Meanwhile, more exotic aeronautical experimentation continued in Mineola. In 1918, large Italian Caproni CA33 bombers were brought in and examined for a possible new heavy bomber for the Air Corps. LePrieur solid fuel rockets were fired from Jennies and assessed for use in destroying enemy observation balloons. These electrically fired rockets were the first rockets fired from an aircraft in America. In 1918, an Aero Medical Laboratory was also extablished at Mineola which performed the earliest American aviation medical experiments. They developed tests for prospective fliers, designed oxygen masks, and rebreathing devices, and built altitude chambers to study the effects of vertigo and lack of oxygen. In 1926, the laboratory was moved from Mitchel Field to Brooks Field, Texas, where it remains to this day.[2]

In April 1917, the Aviation School at Mineola was ordered to revert to its original assignment as a flying school and experimentation there declined. Plans were made to resume flying on a large scale that summer. Long Island remained an important center of aeronautical experimentation through the 1920s with the establishment of the Guggenheim Full Flight Laboratory at Mitchel Field. At the end of 1917, all Air Service testing was shifted to Langley Field, Virginia, where aeronautical experimentation continues today.

In May 1916 the Sheepshead Bay Preparedness Tournament was held at the racetrack in Brooklyn. Prizes were offered to Army aviators to show off this new branch of the service. A Curtiss Twin JN flown by Victor Carlstrom flew nonstop from Newport News, Virginia, to Brooklyn, setting a new American distance record of 416 miles. Another Twin JN also set an altitude record of 14,500 feet with a passenger.

Naval aviation was also developing on Long Island during this same period. In 1917, the Yale Unit was organized by F. Trubee Davison. This group was composed of volunteer college men who wanted to serve and fly in the Navy in World War I. They began their naval aviation training on Curtiss Flying Boats in Huntington Bay at their own expense. By 1918, Naval Air Stations were established at Bay Shore, Montauk Point, and Rockaway Beach.[3]

Aircraft manufacturing also took firm hold on Long Island during World War I. In 1918, the Curtiss Company opened its experimental aircraft factory on the corner of Clinton and Stewart Avenues in Garden City. This was the first factory in the world just for the research and development of aircraft. Glenn Curtiss

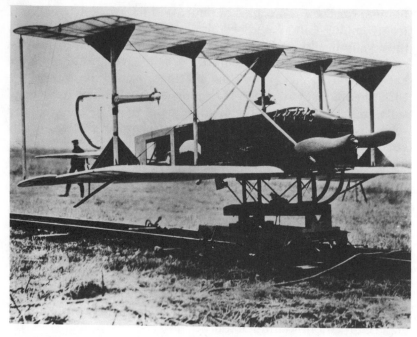

Sperry Aerial Torpedo being tested on railroad tracks, 1918.

personally moved from Buffalo to Garden City to head up the new operation. By the end of World War I, Curtiss had 3,000 employees building, among other things, the giant Navy NC transatlantic flying boats.[4]

After founding the Lawrence Sperry Aircraft Company in 1917, Lawrence Sperry launched the first successful unmanned aircraft in the United States on Long Island in 1918. Five biplane Aerial Torpedoes were built by Curtiss and were flown automatically by Lawrence Sperry's Gyro-Stabilizer off of railroad tracks from Amityville over the Great South Bay. These aircraft were intended to be loaded with explosives and flown into enemy targets. They were never used operationally, but they showed the potential for the development of unmanned aircraft. They can be considered the distant ancestors of today's cruise missiles.[5]

The Breese Aircraft Company was established in Farmingdale in 1917 for the production of Penguin primary training aircraft. The Penguin was intended to give military pilots in basic training the experience of controlling aircraft at near-flight speeds without actually being airborne. Resembling a Bleriot, the wings were too short and the two-cylinder Lawrance engine too small to actually get it airborne, yet they were quite difficult to control in that they had no steerable wheel or brakes. Breese received an order for 300 Penguins at the end of 1917. However, the order was cut back to 250, all being delivered by October 1918. By 1920 all remaining Penguins were scrapped, except for the sole survivor now on display at the Cradle of Aviation Museum on Mitchel Field in Garden City, Long Island. The Penguin's engine was designed by Long Islander Charles Lawrance, who later became the father of the American radial engine. Lawrance was also important in establishing the Wright engine dynasty.

World War I saw the establishment of the aviation industry on Long Island. Several manufacturers who began building aircraft during the war continued building more developed military aircraft in the postwar period. These manufacturers included Sperry, LWF, Orenco, and Curtiss and will be discussed in the following chapter. (Also see the listing of aviation manufacturers in the Appendix for further details.)

A Curtiss JN–4 prepares for a night airmail flight
in the mid-1920s.

The "Golden Age" of Flight

In the 1920s and 1930s, the technology of aircraft underwent a revolution. Flying went from being a dangerous sport to becoming a viable major industry. Aircraft themselves went from being constructed of wood and fabric to steel and aluminum. During the 1920s, aviation began to touch all aspects of American life. The public clearly saw the unprecedented potential of aviation for commercial transport, airmail, aerial advertising, cartography, and sport. All of these trends manifested themselves on Long Island. Approximately 20 Long Island aircraft manufacturers made major contributions to U.S. civil and military aviation during this critical period, thus shaping the aeronautical revolution. The rapid progress of U.S. aviation during the Golden Age can be traced through the Long Island manufacturers, airfields, colorful personalities, and the many record-setting flights that began or ended on Long Island. Long Islanders directly helped in the development of aviation by their experimentation, their courage, and also through their support of aviation by regularly purchasing new planes and thus encouraging the many manufacturers to come up with newer and better designs.

A prime example is airmail, which returned to Long Island at the end of the war. In May 1918, the first regular airmail service was established, when Army fliers inaugurated the run between Washington, D.C. and Belmont Park. Using Curtiss JN-4s, they were the Postal Department's first aircraft. By September 1920, the first transcontinental airmail service was established when the route opened between Curtiss (Roosevelt) Field and San Francisco. Using surplus DH-4s, the route took 83 hours total time. In 1924, the total time was greatly shortened when night airmail flights began. This run took only 40 hours from Curtiss Field to California. Mitchel Field was also the New York airmail terminus when the Army took over airmail service for a brief period in 1934. Thus, airmail service was established on Long Island.

1919—Year of Transatlantic Flight

The year 1919 was an important year for aviation on Long Island. The new, more advanced types of aircraft developed in World War I were being put to use in exciting nonmilitary ways. People seriously began to consider the possibility of flying across the Atlantic Ocean. The technology of aircraft had improved enough during the war that such flights now seemed feasible. Located on the edge of the ocean and next to America's largest city, Long Island was the logical place to begin or end such an aerial voyage. The first attempt at a transatlantic flight, however, did not meet with success. On May 14, 1919, Navy dirigible C-5 made a record flight of 1,115 miles from Montauk to St. Johns, Newfoundland, in 25 hours, 40 minutes, the first leg of an attempted transatlantic flight. However, a severe storm in Newfoundland the next day caused the airship to break loose from its moorings and it disappeared at sea.

At the same time, three huge four-engined Navy Curtiss NC flying boats (aircraft that could only take off and land on water) took off from Rockaway Naval Air Station for a planned flight to Europe. The NC was a Curtiss wartime design, intended to be able to fly to Europe and thus avoid U-boats. After two stops en route, only one of the flying boats, the NC-4 commanded by Lt. Commander Albert Read, reached Portugal, arriving on May 27. This was the historic first flight from America to Europe. The Atlantic was conquered by air. With the future development of aviation, there was no question that the time would come when such flights would be routine.[1]

The first transatlantic airship flight (as well as the first nonstop flight) was when the British dirigible R-34 flew from Scotland to Roosevelt Field. The 600–foot long airship made the leisurely crossing in 108 hours. When it arrived over Roosevelt Field, on July 6, 1919, a crew member parachuted to the ground to organize the large landing crew needed to haul in the huge airship. As the first "rigid" airship in America, it drew tremendous crowds during its stay on Long Island. The R-34 departed on July 9, flew over New York City and landed back in Scotland 75 hours later.[2] Other dirigibles could occasionally be seen over Long Island during the Golden Age. The Naval airship *Shenandoah* conducted the first experiments in which an airship was moored to a ship at sea. It safely docked to a Navy ship in the Long Island Sound in August 1924. The German zeppelin *Hindenburg* also flew over Long Island in 1936 on its many trips to nearby Lakehurst, New Jersey.

In August 1919, the First International Air Race was held from Roosevelt Field to Toronto. This race included both military and civilian pilots flying mostly war surplus U.S., British, and German aircraft. The race, which featured 40 aircraft, was marred by crashes. It was won by Lt. Belvin Maynard in a DH-4 after seven and one-half hours flying time. A transcontinental race was held in October, from Roosevelt Field to San Francisco and back. Marred by seven fatalities en route, the race was won again by Belvin Maynard in his DH-4.[3]

On September 18, Chief Curtiss test pilot Roland Rohlfs set a new world altitude record above Curtiss (Roosevelt) Field. Rohlfs reached the incredible altitude of 34,910 feet—higher than most jets fly today—in his open cockpit Curtiss triplane.

Record-Setting Flights

During this Golden Age of aviation on Long Island, speed, distance, and other record-setting flying became the rage. Almost every year aviators strove to set such new records. The known limits of flight were pushed back regularly in the skies over Long Island.

In May 1923, the first nonstop flight across America was made. Lts. J.S. Macready and O. Kelly took off from Roosevelt Field in a large, single-engine, Fokker T-2 and landed in San Diego 26 hours and 50 minutes later.[4] This record was shortened on June 23, 1924, when Army pilot Russell Maughan flew from Mitchel Field to San Francisco in 21 hours, 48 minutes. The dawn-to-dusk flight, as it was known, was made in a Curtiss Pursuit. The first major solo duration record was set on May 2 and 3, 1928, when Lt. Royal Thomas, in the Bellanca monoplane *Reliance*, remained aloft over Mitchel Field for 35 hours, 25 minutes.

Raymond Orteig, a wealthy New York hotel owner, had offered a prize of $25,000 in 1919 for the first nonstop aircraft flight from New York to Paris. By the mid 1920s, the airplane had developed technically so that nonstop transatlantic flights could be ventured. The first attempt to win the Orteig prize came in September 1926, when World War I Ace Rene Fonck and a crew of three came to Roosevelt Field to try to fly the Atlantic in a big Sikorsky S-35. The heavily loaded ship crashed and burned on takeoff, however, killing two of the crew. Nonetheless, this did nothing to deter interest in the prize as Roosevelt Field became the headquarters for those willing to dare the unknown. Commander Byrd, flushed with success after his North Pole flight, arrived there in the Fokker tri-motor *America.* Clarence Chamberlin was there with the Bellanca monoplane *Miss Columbia,* owned by Charles Levine. The public followed the plans for these flights with intense interest. This interest increased after May 7, 1927, when French aviators Nungesser and Coli disappeared over the Atlantic in an attempt to fly from Paris to New York.

Then a new face quietly flew in from the west. A young airmail pilot, Charles Lindbergh, flying a Ryan monoplane, the *Spirit of St. Louis,* arrived at Curtiss Field on May 12. Lindbergh attracted a great deal of attention while he was there. He was young, a loner, quiet, and the only one attempting to fly the ocean alone in a single-engine plane. In fact, the engine for Lindbergh's Ryan was a Wright J-5, designed by Long Islander Charles Lawrance. Lindbergh waited at the Garden City Hotel until the weather cleared. Lindbergh had stored his Ryan at Curtiss Field, but on the rainy morning of May 20 he had it moved east to Roosevelt Field which had a longer runway. At 7:52 a.m., Lindbergh took off heading east from the muddy runway, heavily loaded with gas and barely clearing the trees. The runway ran east/west through where Fortunoff's parking lot is now, just south of Old Country Road. After a protracted flight of 33 hours and 30 minutes, the exhausted Lindbergh arrived in Paris. This single triumphal event revolutionized aviation. It clearly showed the future potential of aviation and it gave credibility to the civilian flier.[5]

Lindbergh's flight came at precisely the right moment in history. By 1927, aircraft engines were becoming more reliable with better power-to-weight ratios; navigational devices were better too. Lindbergh's achievement caught the world's imagination just when long-range flying became reasonably within reach and the style of the achievement appealed greatly to the public. Although the *Spirit of St. Louis* was of no conceivable use as a

Charles A. Lindbergh, 1927

passenger carrier, people began to think of possibly traveling by air. Lindbergh foresaw this when he wrote in 1927: "The year will surely come when passengers and mail will fly every day from America to Europe." The flight also placed the U.S. aircraft industry into the front line for the first time. The danger and daring of Lindbergh's flight is evidenced by the fact that no one else has flown solo from New York to Paris to this very day.

Within the next few weeks, Chamberlin and Levine flew nonstop to Germany, setting a new distance record. This was followed shortly by Commander Byrd flying nonstop to France. The year 1927 was truly a year of eagles.

The most famous Long Island woman pilot during the Golden Age was Elinor Smith of Freeport. After soloing in 1926 at the age of 15, she went on to set several women's altitude and endurance records over the next three years. In 1928, she became the first and only pilot to fly under all four East River bridges in New York. By 1930, she was voted the best woman pilot in the

Elinor Smith of Freeport, preparing for
another record altitude flight from Roosevelt Field.

United States. Her 1929 women's solo endurance record of 26½
hours stands until this day.[6]

The first ever aerial traffic reports began in 1936. A Goodyear
blimp operating out of Holmes Airport in Queens, broadcast
conditions on the New York area roadways daily to frustrated
drivers.

The Growth of Civilian Airfields on Long Island

After the thrilling success of Lindbergh, the American public
became much more "air-minded," and a wave of flying fever
swept the country. So many people wanted to learn to fly that
several new airfields were established on Long Island just for the
private flier. The most exclusive of these new fields was the
Aviation Country Club, opened in Hicksville in 1929. This was an

elite private flying club which catered to the tastes of wealthy Long Islanders. Charles Lindbergh, Alexander de Seversky, Amelia Earhart, Cornelius Vanderbilt, and Harry Guggenheim among others could be counted among its members. Equipped with their own clubhouse, pool, tennis court, and restaurant, this country club of the air operated until 1950.

One of the best ways to get in on flying cheaply in the post-Lindbergh craze was through gliding, and this too manifested itself on Long Island. In 1929, the Aero Club of Long Island was revived, and its members flew simple primary training gliders from the bluffs at Montauk. This was reputed to be one of the largest glider fields in the United States. Also in 1929, the Peel Glider Boat Corporation began manufacturing low-cost seaplane gliders at its Port Washington plant. Designed to be towed by a boat, these were the first American gliders with a hull. Of the 30 built, the sole survivor is now in the collection of the Cradle of Aviation Museum.[7] By 1930, there was enough gliding activity on Long Island to hold a local gliding meet. The Bayside Glider Meet was held in Queens on May 1 and 2, 1930. Several notables participated including gliding pioneers Hawley Bowlus and Ralph Barnaby. Barnaby flew the same Prufling glider which he later flew from the Navy dirigible *Los Angeles* becoming the first manned aircraft to be launched from a dirigible in flight. The Bayside Glider Meet also had the first U.S. mail carried by a glider.

By far the biggest and most colorful Long Island airfield during the Golden Age was Roosevelt Field. At the end of World War I, Roosevelt Field comprised some 700 acres. In 1919, the western half of the field was sold to the Curtiss Aeroplane and Motor Company and became known as Curtiss Field. The eastern half, east of the gully which later became Meadowbrook Parkway, remained as Roosevelt Field. Most of Curtiss Field was occupied by the Curtiss Flying Service where there was a flying school as well as aircraft sales, service, and flight tests of Curtiss products. Most of the historic flights took place on the eastern field, not where the Roosevelt Field Shopping Center is now. It was on the eastern field that the R-34 landed and all the transatlantic flights embarked. Most of the land of the eastern field was sold in 1935 to become an automobile-racing, and later, horse-racing track. No monument marks the actual location where Lindbergh took off.

Roosevelt Field, circa 1935,
which is now a vacant parking lot.

In 1929, Roosevelt Field Incorporated bought out Curtiss Field and combined the two fields into one large flying area, known as Roosevelt Field. Whereas the eastern field was dirt with only two structures, the western field had paved runways, many concrete hangars, a hotel, restaurant, and was completely equipped for night and instrument flying. At this time it was being called the "World's Premier Airport," and rightfully so. By the mid 1930s Roosevelt Field had become the most technically advanced airfield in the United States. By 1935, the eastern field had been sold to become a racetrack, while the western field, Roosevelt Field, continued as an airfield.

Roosevelt Field was the scene of numerous historic aviation records, even after the era of great flights ended. These included:

• December 29/30, 1921, Lloyd Bertraud and Eddie Stinson set an endurance record of 26 hours, 17 minutes in a Junkers-Larsen JL-6.

• February 4 & 5, 1929, Captain Frank Hawks set a new transcontinental west-east speed record, flying from Los Angeles to Roosevelt Field in 18 hours, 21 minutes.

• March 27 & 28, 1929, Martin Jensen set a solo endurance record of 35 hours, 33 minutes.

- April 23 & 24, 1929, Elinor Smith set a women's solo endurance record of 26 hours, 30 minutes.
- March 10, 1930, Elinor Smith set a women's altitude record, 27,418 feet.
- April 20, 1930, Charles and Anne Morrow Lindbergh set a new transcontinental speed record, California to Roosevelt Field in 14 hours, 23 minutes.
- June 27, 1930, Frank Hawks set a new east-west speed record, Roosevelt Field to Los Angeles in 19 hours, 10 minutes.
- August 13–14, 1930, Frank Hawks broke the previous record, crossing the country in 12 hours, 25 minutes.
- April 10, 1931, Elinor Smith set a new women's altitude record of 33,213 feet.
- June 23, 1931, Wiley Post and Harold Gatty set an around-the-world speed record from Roosevelt Field in a Lockheed Vega *Winnie Mae*. They circled the globe in 8 days, 15 hours, 51 minutes.
- October 1933, a National Charity Air Pageant was held at Roosevelt Field and was attended by more than 250,000 visitors, making it Long Island's largest air show to date. At the show, Alexander de Seversky set a new amphibian speed record of 177 mph, in his SEV-3.

In the early 1930s, Roosevelt Field was the largest and busiest civil airfield in the United States. Over 450 planes were based there with up to 400 takeoffs or landings per hour. The field featured regular weekend airshows that drew huge crowds. People flocked from all over Long Island to see aerial acrobatics, skydiving, and precision bombing or to get their first airplane rides. There were 150 aviation businesses on the field with 20 different aircraft sales agencies represented. Anyone on the east coast of the U.S. who wanted to buy a plane, came to Roosevelt Field. The field was also the home of the Roosevelt Aviation School, one of the largest civil flying schools in the United States. Other activity on the field typified the growth and possibility of aviation. There was the American Skywriting Corporation, the first skywriting company in America which used World War I SE-5 fighters, and pioneered the field of aerial advertising. "Voice of the Sky" company advertised from the sky using loudspeakers. Fairchild Aerial Surveys and News Planes demonstrated the use of flying for cartography and documenting history. Roosevelt

Field was an aviation mecca, the home or port of call for virtually every aviator of note during this period.

When World War II arrived, the Navy took over Roosevelt Field and used it as a modification and shipping center for aircraft going overseas. Hundreds of Brewster Buffalos, Vought Corsairs, and Grumman F4Fs replaced the colorful biplanes of the Golden Age. The Roosevelt Aviation School also shifted to the training of mechanics for the Navy. As World War II wound down, so did the history of Roosevelt Field. Private flying tapered off greatly and the field was too far from Manhattan to be commercially successful. Furthermore, the field was providing little tax revenue. Developments were being built around it and the last thing the new homeowners wanted was a major airfield in their backyard. In 1951 the field was closed and sold for development and by 1957 a shopping mall opened on the site.[8]

The Curtiss Flying Service, formerly of Garden City, moved to a new airport in Valley Stream in 1929. This new airfield, Curtiss Field, physically the largest civilian field on Long Island, had the misfortune to open just as the Depression struck. It was to be a major aviation center, but was forced to close in 1933 due to the Depression. However, during its brief history, several important events happened at Curtiss Field. In November 1929, a Russian Tupolev *Land of the Soviets* arrived in Valley Stream, completing a transglobal flight from Moscow with several stops in between. A huge crowd, including Charles Lindbergh, was on hand to greet the Russian fliers. In September 1930, French aviators Coste and Bellonte landed here after a flight from Paris.

The history of Curtiss Field, Valley Stream, is perhaps best associated with that of early women aviators. In 1929, the first organization of women pilots was established here, known as the "Ninety-Nines" (named after the number of original members). Amelia Earhart, present at the group's initial meeting was elected the organization's first president. The Ninety-Nines remain in existence to this day and are currently a global organization of women pilots.[9] Louise Thaden and Frances Marsalis set a women's world refueled endurance record of 8 days, 4 hours leaving from and returning to Valley Stream in August 1932.

Aeronautical activity was revived at Curtiss Field during World War II when Columbia Aircraft produced J2F Duck

Amphibians, with postwar production of civilian Skyrangers continuing until 1946. By the late 1940s the field was completely closed, the site sold to become another ubiquitous shopping mall (now Green Acres).

Long Island's Military Airfields

Not only was Long Island the center of tremendous civil aviation activity during the Golden Age, but it was also home to one of the largest U.S. military airfields at that time. Mitchel Field continued to grow after World War I and between 1929 and 1932 a major new construction program was undertaken. New brick barracks, officers' clubs, housing, warehouses, and operations buildings were constructed, as well as eight massive steel and concrete hangars. Much of this construction remains in place today. Between the wars Mitchel was the Army's premier Air Corps base, somewhat of a military Country Club atmosphere with fine housing, clubs, pools, polo fields, and tree-lined streets. It became home to several observation, fighter, and bombardment groups and it hosted the 1920 and 1925 National Air Races. The 1920 Pulitzer Race saw Major C.S. Mosely set a new speed record of 156 mph, while in 1925 Lt. Cyrus Bettis set another world speed record of 249 mph in a Long Island built Curtiss Racer. In 1922, the Army laid out its first air route, a model airway, from Mitchel Field to McCook Field, Ohio. In 1938, Mitchel was the starting point for the first nonstop transcontinental bomber flight, made by Army B-18s. Mitchel Field also served as a base from which the first demonstration of long-range aerial reconnaissance was made. In May 1939, three B-17s led by Lt. Curtiss Lemay flew 750 miles out to sea and intercepted the Italian ocean liner *Rex*. This was a striking example of the range, mobility, and accuracy of modern aviation at the time.

During World War II, Mitchel was the main point of air defense for New York City, equipped with two squadrons of P-40 fighters. In the late 1940s it was headquarters of the Air Defense Command, First Air Force and Continental Air Command. By 1949, Mitchel was relieved of the responsibility for defending New York City because of the many problems associated with operating tactical aircraft in an urban area. However, Mitchel did serve as the terminus for the last speed record set on Long Island, a transcontinental speed record of 4 hours, 8 minutes set by Col. W. Millikan in an F-86 on January 2, 1954. After several notable crashes, including a P-47 into Hofstra University's Barnard Hall, public pressure ultimately led to the field's closure. The last active unit to be based at Mitchel was the 514th Troop Carrier Wing flying Fairchild C-119 Flying Boxcars. Due to the noise, small size of the field, and several spectacular crashes, Mitchel was closed in 1961 with the property being turned over to the County of Nassau.

Perhaps the most historic and important work accomplished on Mitchel Field was done by the Guggenheim Full Flight Laboratory in 1929 and 1930. In the mid 1920s Long Islander Harry Guggenheim, a friend of Charles Lindbergh, became interested in funding a laboratory concerned with making flying safer. Thus the Full Flight Laboratory was established at Mitchel Field. Its first project was to study ways of safely flying at night and in bad weather. Lt. James Doolittle was selected to carry out the experiments at Mitchel. Working with the Sperry Gyroscope Company and Pioneer Instrument Company of Brooklyn, and the Kollsman Company of Queens, they developed new instruments that would allow an aircraft to navigate and land solely on instruments alone. By the summer of 1929, Doolittle outfitted a Consolidated NY-2 Husky with the necessary equipment. On September 24, 1929, Doolittle climbed into the plane and closed a special cockpit covering so he had no vision outside the cockpit. He then took off from Mitchel, flew a prescribed course and landed, flying solely on instruments. It was the world's first "blind flight" and it helped make aviation as safe as it is today. Within a year, blind flying equipment was installed in most airmail and commercial planes. The first transcontinental blind flight was also made from Mitchel Field in June 1936. On June 7, Major Ira Eaker piloted his Boeing P-12 across country solely on instruments.

In 1930, the Guggenheim Laboratory concerned itself with the development of an aircraft incorporating as many safety features as possible, especially those concerned with low speed handling. It initiated the 1930 Guggenheim Safe Aircraft Competition with a $100,000 prize. This competition was won by a Long Island built Curtiss Tanager over many competitors. The Tanager incorporated many advanced concepts such as leading edge slats (devices which increase lift at low speed) and trailing edge flaps for low speed takeoffs and landings. To this day, all jet airliners include such features. Great technical strides in aviation were made on Long Island.[10]

The Need for Commercial Airports

As aviation in America expanded rapidly during the Golden Age so too did aviation on Long Island and around the New York area in general. The lack of a major airport within the city limits resulted in the loss of the lucrative airmail contract to Newark Airport. New York City took steps to rectify this situation in the late 1920s. The site chosen for New York's official airport was in the marshes of Jamaica Bay, Long Island. By 1931, Floyd Bennett Field (named after Admiral Byrd's pilot), New York's first municipal airport, opened on Barren Island on the south shore of Brooklyn. In spite of the many fine new hangars and administrative buildings, airlines were still reluctant to move from Newark due to the lack of rail and direct highway connection from Floyd Bennett Field to Manhattan. Nonetheless, with the opening of this newer, larger airport closer to New York City, most historic flight activity shifted from Roosevelt Field to Floyd Bennett Field. The following historic flights occurred at this new airport:

- February 1931, Ruth Nichols in a Lockheed Vega set a world altitude record for diesel-powered aircraft, nearly 20,000 feet.
- July 1931, Russell Boardman and John Polando in a Bellanca monoplane flew to Istanbul in 43 hours setting a new nonstop distance record.
- July 1933, the largest air armada to ever visit the U.S. arrived at Floyd Bennett. Italian General Italo Balbo led a flight of 24 Savoia-Marchetti flying boats.
- July 1933, Wiley Post set off from Floyd Bennett for a solo around-the-world flight. Assisted by the new Sperry Autopilot, he returned in 7 days, 18 hours to set a new world record.
- August 1933, Paul Codos and Maurice Rossi in a Bleriot 110 flew to Syria establishing a world nonstop distance record of 5,637 miles.
- September 1936, Louise Thaden and Blanche Noyes in a Beechcraft won the Bendix Trophy, flying from Floyd Bennett to Los Angeles in nearly 16 hours.

- July 1938, Howard Hughes and four others in a Lockheed Vega set an around-the-world speed record from Floyd Bennett, 3 days, 19 hours.

In July 1938, the most bizarre Long Island flight took place. Douglas Corrigan, just in from Roosevelt Field, took off from Floyd Bennett Field for a purported nonstop flight to California. Flying a nine-year-old Curtiss Robin, clearly in poor condition and lacking a radio and all other modern instruments, Corrigan arrived the next day in Ireland claiming he had simply flown the "wrong way." Corrigan became an instant national celebrity and was warmly welcomed upon his arrival back at Roosevelt Field. This wasn't an historic pathfinding flight like Lindbergh's, but it did give America a good laugh while in the midst of the Depression.

Due to the lack of commercial success and rising international tension, the Navy took over Floyd Bennett Field in 1941. During the war the field was home to Navy Fleet Service Squadrons, Cadet Flight Training, Ferry Command, Military Air Transport Command, and base for antisubmarine patrols. The field remained a Naval Air Station until it closed in 1970.

By the late 1930s, commercial air transportation was booming with more planes connecting more cities and with more passengers flying all the time. As the newer planes had greater range, commercial transatlantic flights became feasible for the first time. The first regular commercial transatlantic airline service was initiated at Port Washington on Long Island's north shore in 1937. Huge Pan-American Boeing and Martin flying boats departed and arrived with regularity from Manhasset Bay for the next two years.

However, New York City was still dissatisfied with its airport situation so in the late 1930s construction began on a new commercial airport located on the site of the old, small, Glenn Curtiss airport at North Beach, Queens. Heavy landfill created a much larger airport, located on a main highway, near a subway line, and closer to the city with unobstructed water approaches. Completed under a $40 million WPA project, the new airport opened in October 1939 as New York Municipal Airport. However, in the 1940s it simply came to be known as LaGuardia, named after the popular mayor who pushed it through to completion. During 1939 all commercial flying boat activity was moved from Port Washington to the new Marine Air Terminal at LaGuardia. During the early 1940s LaGuardia became the busiest airport in the country. It recorded 197,000 flights for 1946 alone. LaGuardia has been enlarged several times since in order to handle increased jet traffic, but most of the original hangars and other buildings still survive.

Needing yet a larger airport to handle larger, faster planes and more traffic, New York City opened Idlewild Airport on the shores of Jamaica Bay in 1948. This new field had much more room for expansion than all other airports in the greater New York area. This airport was eventually to be known as John F. Kennedy International.

Long Island's Aviation Manufacturers

During the Golden Age there were more aviation manufacturers on Long Island than in any other area of the country. This was due to the number of good military and civilian flying fields and the close proximity of New York for financial backing. Each contributed to the development of aviation in its own way. Unfortunately, today only one aircraft manufacturer remains on Long Island. The rest went bankrupt during the Depression, or moved to sunnier and less expensive locations. In addition to the manufacturers mentioned here, there were numerous smaller ones who only produced one or two unsuccessful aircraft. However, the building of aircraft on Long Island has been continuous since aviation's earliest days when inventors built frail biplanes in their backyards.

After World War I Lawrence Sperry continued the development of aircraft at the Sperry Company in Farmingdale. Sperry's first major aircraft contract, in 1921, was for the construction of 42 Sperry Messengers for the Army Air Corps. In 1922 they produced the Sperry-Verville R-3 Racer, the most advanced monoplane of the postwar period and the first with retractable landing gear. The company dissolved in 1923, shortly after Lawrence Sperry's untimely death, when his Messenger crashed in the English Channel. The Sperry Gyrosope Company of Brooklyn, owned by Lawrence's father Elmer, continued on Long Island, eventually establishing divisions in Great Neck and Lake Success.[11]

The LWF Engineering Company of Long Island City was established in 1915 by Edward Lowe, Charles Willard, and Robert Fowler to manufacture aircraft fuselages of Willard's design. In 1916 they moved to College Point and built a total of 45 aircraft of their own design. Since most of their planes were sold to the military, LWF ceased operation after World War I in 1923.[12]

In 1912 Vincent Burnelli built his first aircraft, a glider, in Brooklyn. In 1917 he built his first powered aircraft. By 1924 Burnelli had built the RB-2 which is generally recognized as being the first air freighter. Although comparatively few Burnelli aircraft were built, but his ideas had some impact on the subsequent development of aviation.[13]

The Ordnance Engineering Company (Orenco) was established in Baldwin in 1917, primarily for aeronautical contracting with the Air Service. Before they went bankrupt in 1922 due to the lack of postwar military sales, they built a total of 22 aircraft, all for the Air Corps.

In 1918, the Curtiss Company, headquartered in Buffalo split its work effort and shifted all aircraft research and development to

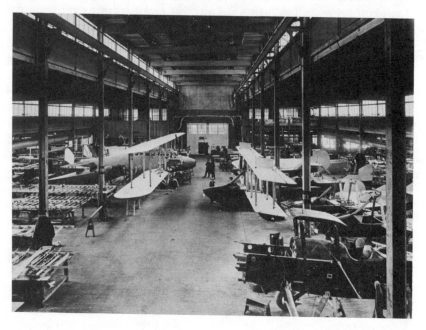

Interior of the Curtiss Factory, Garden City, circa 1920.

Long Island in order to separate it from the mass-production in Buffalo. Glenn Curtiss chose the Garden City site for their new experimental plant because of its accessibility to Hazelhurst Field. This was the first aircraft factory in the world to concentrate on new designs, rather than production. Between 1918 and 1930, Curtiss developed some of the best-known aircraft of the Golden Age on Long Island. The Curtiss Garden City plant also possessed the only corporate-owned wind tunnel in America. In 1931, the Garden City plant closed and its operations were moved back to Buffalo. However, the building still stands on the corner of Clinton and Stewart Avenues. It is one of the oldest surviving aircraft factories in the world, if not the oldest.[14]

The Vought Corporation was founded in 1920 by designer Chance Vought, primarily as a contractor for the U.S. Navy. Vought produced approximately 200 aircraft in their Long Island City factory. By 1923 Vought was the largest supplier of aircraft to the U.S. Navy, but in 1929 the corporation moved to Hartford, Connecticut.[15]

Cox-Klemin was established in 1921 at College Point by L. C. Cox and well-known aeronautical engineer Alexander Klemin. In 1924 the company moved to Baldwin, taking over the old Orenco factory. In all, they produced a total of only 16 aircraft; however, these included several notable types. Perhaps Cox-Klemin is best known for producing the tiny XS-1, the first aircraft to be launched from a submarine. Built for the Navy in 1923, it could easily be folded and stored below deck, By 1925, however, Cox-Klemin was out of business due to minimal aircraft sales in the postwar period.

Sikorsky was established in 1923 by Soviet emigré designer Igor Sikorsky. Their first airplane was the S-29, a twin-engine biplane, which was built in a small building in Roosevelt. The Sikorsky Aviation Corporation moved to College Point in Queens in 1926 to continue the successful development of amphibious aircraft. Sikorsky built a total of 65 aircraft on Long Island. The company moved to Bridgeport, Connecticut in 1929 and is still in business today.[16]

Fairchild was established in 1925 in Farmingdale specifically for the manufacture of large, single-engine, monoplane photographic aircraft. Fairchild's 1928 Model 71 cabin monoplane was by far their most successful product with 200 being built. A 1928

Fairchild FC-2, the *Stars and Stripes,* was used by Admiral Byrd on his 1929 and 1934 Antarctic expeditions. Fairchild built a total of 369 planes on Long Island before moving to Maryland in 1931, although their Ranger Aircraft Engine Division remained in Farmingdale until operations ceased with the end of World War II.[17]

EDO was founded at College Point in 1925 by Earl D. Osborne. The company manufactured a new product—all-metal aircraft floats. By 1929 they were manufacturing eight models of floats and the workforce reached 100. During World War II, EDO produced all the floats for U. S. Naval aircraft. Today EDO continues making aircraft floats in its College Point factory. They also make sophisticated electronic equipment.[18]

The Ireland Aircraft Company was founded at Roosevelt Field in 1926 by Sumner Ireland. Ireland is noted for making the first serious attempt at developing the modern personal amphibian. All construction was done in the hangars at Curtiss/ Roosevelt Field with 100 men building two planes per month. Ireland, reorganized as Amphibions Inc. in 1930, built a total of 39 aircraft before the Depression caused their bankruptcy in 1932.[19]

Brunner-Winkle was established in Glendale, Queens in 1928 to build the "Bird" biplane. In production from 1928 to 1931, the Bird was a fairly successful private aircraft in its day. Final assembly and flight test of the Bird was at Roosevelt Field. A total of 239 Brunner-Winkle Birds were built before the Depression forced the company into bankruptcy in 1932.[20]

American Aeronautical Corporation was established in Port Washington in 1928 to manufacture, under license, the well-known line of Italian Savoia-Marchetti flying boats and amphibians. This was the only Long Island aircraft manufacturing company building a foreign design. They built 36 S-56 three-seat, open cockpit biplane amphibians between 1929 and 1931. In 1931, the Depression and subsequent slow sales forced the company into bankruptcy. However, their Port Washington hangar/factory survives on the eastern shore of Manhasset Bay.[21]

The American Airplane & Engine Corporation was formed in 1931 to build aircraft and engines in the former Fairchild plant in Farmingdale. It was only in business for less than two years during which they produced 27 "Pilgrim" aircraft.

Organized in 1932 in Long Island City, the Brewster Aeronautical Corporation was the successor to the Brewster Company that had previously built carriages, automobiles, and later floats for Vought Corsairs. In 1936 the company produced its first aircraft, the SBA Scout Bomber. This all-metal monoplane design established Brewster's credibility with the Navy which soon placed an order for their new fighter—the F2A Buffalo for the Navy. Needing room for large-scale production, they moved into an old automobile factory in Long Island City which was the only vertical aircraft factory in the world. All final assembly and flight testing was done at Roosevelt Field. In all, approximately 550 Buffalos were built. Brewster was known as the first U.S. aircraft manufacturing company to hire large numbers of black employees for production, a move which was unpopular in 1940, but a credit to their management. Brewster also has the dubious distinction of being the only U.S. defense contractor to experience a strike during World War II (1943). Due to lagging production and cash flow problems, the Navy took over direct management of Brewster in 1942. The company was liquidated in 1945 as military aircraft production needs were limited after the end of the war.[22]

The Loening Aircraft Company was founded in Mineola in 1932 by famed aeronautical engineer Grover Loening. Loening

Most Long Island aircraft manufacturers produced seaplanes or amphibians at some point in their history. This Grumman G-21 Goose served as a pilot training aircraft for Pan American Airways at North Beach (LaGuardia) Airport, Queens, in the early 1940s.

started the Long Island plant to do experimental and development work with amphibians which he had built successfully in New York City. Only four amphibians were built at Mineola, however, none going into production.

Columbia was established in 1943 at Curtiss Field, Valley Stream, primarily to produce Grumman J2F-6 Ducks under subcontract from Grumman. The Duck was a biplane amphibian that was extensively used in World War II as a utility, transport, and rescue aircraft. In all, Columbia built 330 Ducks. In 1946 Columbia was sold to Commonwealth Aircraft of Kansas City and for that year they produced the Skyranger two-seat civil aircraft. Due to the lack of a postwar civil aircraft market, construction of Skyrangers was suspended in 1947 and the company ceased all operations.

The two largest Long Island aircraft manufacturers, Grumman and Republic, also had their start in the Golden Age, but most of their production occurred during World War II. They will be discussed in the next section.

World War II—Long Island, Arsenal of Freedom

There is no question that Long Island built aircraft and other related products that helped America and its Allies achieve victory in World War II. Allied fighter operations were clearly dominated by Long Island built airplanes. Starting with several small, stable companies, the demands of war brought tremendous growth in the aircraft industry on Long Island. In fact, by 1945, over 100,000 people worked in the aviation industry on Long Island.

In addition to aircraft manufacturing, there was also a large amount of military activity on Long Island during the war. The Navy operated Roosevelt Field as an aircraft modification and shipping center. Floyd Bennett Field was also a major Naval aviation base. Mitchel Field was the Air Defense Center for New York City during the war. In 1940, two squadrons of P-40s were transferred in to provide fighter protection for the city. A squadron of B-25 medium bombers was also stationed at Mitchel and their first wartime antisubmarine patrol was flown on December 8, 1941. During the course of the war, field activity increased so dramatically that Mitchel was one of the largest Air Corps bases in the United States. Mitchel became the jumping off point for bomber squadrons going to Europe and for wounded men coming back.

Many Long Islanders wanting to do their part during the war joined the Civil Air Patrol. Large Civil Air Patrol Squadrons were established at Westhampton Beach and Roosevelt Field in 1942. These groups flew daily antisubmarine missions for the next three years. Flying mostly civilian Stinsons and Wacos, equipped with bombs, Coastal Air Patrol (CAP) Base 17 at Westhampton Beach patrolled the ocean coast from Rhode Island to New York Harbor. It was one of the largest CAP bases in the United States.

Many Long Island women also entered the workforce for the

Mitchel Field, and in upper left, Roosevelt Field, circa 1940.

first time during the war. Due to drastically increased production and a shortage of labor, thousands of women went to work at Grumman, Republic, Brewster, and Sperry for the duration of the war. Though previously a male-dominated field, over 40 percent of the defense workforce on Long Island by the end of the war were women. Other Long Island women served as Women's Air Service Pilots (WASPS) who ferried American fighters and bombers across the country and to Europe.

During the war, the Sperry Company moved from Brooklyn to Lake Success. They built many important components for U.S. aircraft, including artificial horizons, bombsights, automatic pilots, radars, gunsights, and armor-plated ball turrets for B-17s and B-24s. Sperry expanded rapidly during the war and had some 22,000 employees at its peak. Columbia Aircraft in Valley Stream was producing J2F Ducks for the Navy, Brewster in Queens was producing F2A Buffalos, and Ranger in Farmingdale was producing six-cylinder and V-12 engines for several types of aircraft.

Two smaller companies, Dade Brothers in Mineola and General Aircraft in Queens produced over 700 of the massive wood, steel, and fabric Waco CG-4 Troop Gliders. This type of glider was used to land 14 troops plus equipment behind enemy lines, and was extensively used during the D-Day invasion. Dade Brothers also crated and shipped thousands of American aircraft overseas from Roosevelt Field. This included such diverse types as Brewster F2A, Grumman F4F, Curtiss P-40, Vultee P-66, Republic P-47, and Waco CG-4.

In an interesting sidelight, the name "Long Island" was also recorded in the history books in another way during World War II. The first small escort aircraft carrier ever built was named the USS *Long Island* (CVE-1). This carrier delivered the first Grumman F4Fs directly into the battle of Guadalcanal. The carrier survived the war but was sold and scrapped in Amsterdam in 1974.

The most aeronautical and manufacturing activity on Long Island during the war was by its two largest employers, Grumman and Republic. Grumman continues as Long Island's largest, private employer until this day, while Republic ceased operations in 1987. What follows is a brief history of these two companies from their inception through World War II.

Republic Aviation Corporation

The year 1931 was not the best for starting a new business. Before the year was out, over 28,000 commercial firms failed and countless others foundered. Yet this was the year Soviet emigré Alexander de Seversky founded the Seversky Aircraft Corporation. The company's first plane was a highly streamlined amphibian, the SEV-3, built at their College Point plant, which served as a demonstrator to interest investors in the new firm. The amphibian set several speed records, showed enough promise, and lured sufficient backers so that, by 1936, there were over 1,000 stockholders. In the mid 1930s, Seversky sold several versions of the amphibian to foreign governments and the basic design was modified into a trainer in an attempt to procure a contract from the U.S. Government. In 1935, they were successful and Seversky made its first U.S. sale of BT-8 trainers to the Air Corps.

Seversky's most profitable sale was in 1936 when the Air Corps purchased 77 of their fast, streamlined P-35 fighters. In 1937, Frank Fuller won the Bendix Trophy Race flying a version of the P-35, and famed aviatrix Jackie Cochran also set several speed records in them. With the new P-35 contract, Seversky moved into new larger facilities in Farmingdale. However, in the prewar years, all Seversky's promotional schemes sold only about 140 aircraft, including 100 to the Air Corps. In 1938, the company was forced to seek additional funds to complete its U.S. Army orders and to continue research and development on new designs which would be needed to obtain future orders—a situation that never changed until the last days of the company.

Rising tension in Europe and worldwide rearmament greatly benefitted the firm. The last P-35 built was modified into a new design, the XP-41, which attracted the Air Corps' interest. However, the cost of developing this design drove the company further into debt. At the end of 1938, while Seversky was in England seeking new aircraft orders, the Board of Directors, angered at the bleak financial prospects for the company, voted him out as president and reorganized the company as the Republic Aviation Corporation. The company's situation began to improve rapidly.

Sweden purchased a quantity of P-35s and Republic posted

its first profit in 1939. The great U.S. defense buildup initiated in 1940 spurred additional purchases as the Air Corps ordered $56 million worth of Republic's new P-43 Lancer fighters. In 1941, experimental work began on a new, more advanced fighter, the P-47 Thunderbolt, which had more speed, power, range, and load-carrying ability than any other U.S. fighter. In May 1941, the XP-47, the first U.S. fighter to travel 400 mph, had its maiden flight. The Air Corps immediately placed a large order for P-47s and within one year Republic Aviation became the second largest supplier of fighter aircraft to the Army Air Corps.

By 1944, Republic had 24,000 employees (up from 5,500 in 1941). They were now the largest producer of fighter aircraft in the world. Republic produced almost 10,000 P-47s with 28 planes per day coming off the assembly lines at one point—more than one per hour! Sales in 1944 came to over $370 million. During World War II, the P-47 was the main Air Corps fighter in Europe. They are credited with destroying over 4,000 enemy planes and 9,000 locomotives. Serving in the fighter/bomber role, the P-47 established a 5:1 "kill ratio" in the skies over Europe (5 enemy planes shot down for each P-47 destroyed). The two leading American aces in Europe, Bob Johnson and Frances Gabreski, both flew the P-47.

As World War II was winding down, Republic saw the need to produce something other than military aircraft. They initiated a project for a civilian amphibious aircraft, the Seabee, which was intended for the anticipated large postwar civil aircraft market. Republic wanted to exploit the private aircraft market the way the automobile market was exploited after World War I. The Seabee was designed to be built quickly and cheaply. There was only one problem—the postwar civil aircraft market never materialized and Republic lost money on the 1,000 Seabees it built. An original Seabee, as well as a P-47, is on display at the Cradle of Aviation Museum.

At the end of the war Republic also was working on an experimental high-speed, long-range photo reconnaissance aircraft, the XR-12 Rainbow. It still holds the speed record for multi-engine, propeller-driven aircraft. The surrender of Germany and Japan, however, led to rapid demobilization in the United States. Once the war ended, the Air Force no longer had a need for such a plane, so production was halted after only two were built.[1]

Courtesy Grumman Corporation

Women aircraft workers assembling Grumman
TBF Avengers in Bethpage, 1943.

Grumman Aircraft Engineering Corporation

The Grumman Aircraft Engineering Corporation, led by Leroy Grumman, opened for business in a garage in Baldwin on January 2, 1930. Their first production contract, for $37,000, was to design and build a single float with retractable landing gear to be tested on one of the Navy's Vought Corsair biplanes. The Navy was pleased with the design, and thus ordered additional floats from Grumman.

Due in large part to the Navy's satisfaction with their floats, in 1931 Grumman won its first contract to build 27 new airplanes. Designated the FF-1, it was built to carry two. It was the first Navy fighter to use retractable landing gear, thus making it faster than any Navy single-seater then in service. Needing more space to produce both floats and aircraft, Grumman moved first into an abandoned Navy reserve hangar at Curtiss Field in Valley Stream (1931), and later into a "real factory" in Farmingdale (1932). The FF-1 design led to a line of Navy biplane fighters that included the F2F and F3F. When the Navy ordered 55 F2Fs, it was their biggest aircraft order since 1918. The mass-produced (160) F3F was the Navy's last biplane fighter, which was produced until 1939. It was also the biggest Naval aircraft order to date. One specially modified F3F, the Gulfhawk, gained fame as it was flown around the country by aerobatic pilot Al Williams.

During the mid 1930s, Grumman entered the amphibian field with the Duck series, which became the Navy's workhorses of World War II. Over 270 were built, making this Grumman's most successful aircraft to date. Later in the 1930s, the company built the amphibious Goose for airline, executive, or military use, many of which are still flying today. Later came the Widgeon, Mallard, and the Albatross for the Coast Guard, Navy, and Air Force. Thus Grumman became one of the world's leading producers of amphibious aircraft.

Grumman made its last move, from Farmingdale to Bethpage in 1937, and they continued the development of a new fighter—the F4F Wildcat. An all-metal monoplane, the F4F was another in the line of Grumman's small, stubby fighters. Built between 1937 and 1945, it formed the backbone of Naval fighter forces early in World War II. The F4F incorporated a revolutionary folding-wing design which permitted more aircraft to be stored on aircraft carriers. During the war, Wildcats established a 7:1 kill ratio over Japanese aircraft and served in the Atlantic for antisubmarine patrol. By 1943, F4F production was shifted to General Motors in order to free Grumman for F6F production. In all, almost 8,000 Wildcats were built.

In 1940, Grumman had approximately 2,000 employees, but by 1941, with war approaching, Congress ordered a buildup of 10,000 military aircraft and for Grumman, as others, the floodgates were suddenly wide open. With the government building new plants at Grumman, the workforce soon more than tripled, and around-the-clock production became a way of life. Using a high percentage of women workers, the F6F Hellcat, the best naval fighter of World War II, rolled off Grumman's assembly lines in record numbers, as did the TBF Avenger. The torpedo/bomber Avenger was the biggest and heaviest carrier aircraft of World War II. They were highly successful in destroying enemy naval and land targets, and future U.S. President George Bush was among the Avenger pilots. A Grumman Hellcat, Avenger, Wildcat, and Goose are currently on display at the Cradle of Aviation Museum.

Between December 7, 1941 (attack on Pearl Harbor) and August 14, 1945 (victory in Japan), Grumman's 24,000 employees delivered a record 17,013 aircraft, more than any other U.S. manufacturer. At one point in 1945, Grumman was turning out more than one plane an hour, 664 in one month, an aircraft production record which has never been equalled. Grumman's F6F established a remarkable kill ratio of 19:1 over Japanese aircraft. Navy records show that Grumman planes accounted for two-thirds of all enemy aircraft destroyed over the Pacific during World War II—a total of almost 6,000 Japanese planes.

Grumman also developed the XF5F-1 Skyrocket during the war, a twin-engine Naval fighter. Although it set a climb record, the XF5F-1 had stability and visibility problems, so no orders were forthcoming. With the end of World War II and rapid demobilization, Grumman's backlog of $380 million worth of orders was cut by a whopping 80 percent. Forseeing the need to diversify out of military aviation, Grumman began the manufacture of aluminum truck bodies and canoes, and this was the basis of these successful product lines that continue today.

Courtesy Grumman Corporation

Hellcats at Grumman in 1945.

In 1944, Grumman built a small, civil aircraft for the predicted postwar personal plane market. Although their Kitten proved a successful flier, a survey revealed there would be few sales for a personal plane costing $7,000, which was the price of a Levittown house in 1947. Only one Kitten was produced, and every manufacturer who attempted to enter the postwar civil aircraft market, such as Republic, lost money.

Grumman was also producing two new Navy fighters just as the war was ending. They built 350 twin-engine F7F Tigercats, although an order for 1,400 was cancelled at the end of the war. Some saw action as Marine night-fighters in Korea. Grumman's last prop-driven fighter, the F8F Bearcat, also appeared at the same time. Lighter and faster than the F6F, it soon proved to be the world's fastest piston engine aircraft, but it was too late to see combat. Grumman built 1,263 for the peacetime Navy, but orders for over 5,000 were terminated in August 1945.

All together, Long Island aircraft manufacturers produced nearly 30,000 aircraft and thousands of other important pieces of aviation equipment for the Allied war effort.

Opening day, Idlewild Field control tower, 1948.

The Postwar Era: The Jet Age

The end of World War II brought the widespread cancellations of military production contracts to many companies on Long Island. At the same time, the rapid population growth in Nassau County let to the forced closing of several airfields, principally historic Roosevelt and Mitchel Fields. The advent of new technology, particularly jet aircraft, further revolutionized aviation and once again placed Long Island in the forefront.

Long Island's Airports

Since 1909, over 80 airports were established on Long Island. Today, however, few remain and none at all on the Hempstead Plains. In the postwar period, the airports at LaGuardia and Idlewild were greatly expanded. Three other airports, Westhampton, Republic, and Islip-MacArthur, established themselves as major facilities.

In February 1946, the first scheduled transatlantic flight was made from the runways at LaGuardia, when a Pan Am Lockheed Constellation flew to England in 12 hours. The airport was expanded several times in the 1950s and in 1963 the first commercial jet, a Boeing 727 landed at LaGuardia.

The first commercial transatlantic jet flight also left from Long Island, when a Pan Am Boeing 707 flew from Idlewild to London in seven and one-half hours in September 1958. During the 1950s, Idlewild became the first large-scale international airport. It not only possessed the world's tallest control tower, but its six operations per minute ranked it as one of the world's busiest airports. Consisting of over 5,000 acres, it is as large as Manhattan from the Battery to 42nd Street. The International Arrivals Building opened in 1957, and by 1985 the airport was handling 25 million passengers per year. Idlewild was rededicated as John F. Kennedy International Airport in 1963 and has been expanded several times since.

Westhampton Beach was established in 1931 as a small civilian field. It expanded tremendously during World War II when it became a gunnery training base for fighter pilots flying P-47s. After World War II, the Air Force took over the installation and the 118th Fighter Squadron flying P-47s was stationed there. The base was at its peak during the 1950s when it became a major Air Defense Base for New York City. There was a tremendous amount of new construction on the field as housing and all other support structures were built to handle the influx of Air Force personnel. Between 1955 and 1969, the 52nd Fighter Group was stationed there, flying F-86D Sabres at first, and later F-102 Delta Daggers, and lastly F-101 Voodoos. Between 1959 and 1964, the 6th Air Defense Missile Squadron was based at Westhampton Beach, using Bomarc missiles for air defense. Long Island was given such importance that this was the first air defense missile base established in the United States. The Air Force Base closed in 1969, and the field was turned over to the county. Today Westhampton continues as a small general aviation airport. However, it still houses the 106th Air Refueling and Rescue Unit, the only remaining active Air Force Unit on Long Island. Thus this last unit is the final page in the history of military aviation on Long Island, dating from 1915.

Republic Airport in Farmingdale was founded in 1928 as Fairchild Flying Field. Since then the field has housed several manufacturers including Fairchild, Grumman, Seversky, and Ranger. Republic, which owned the field, continued building aircraft there until 1987. The field first opened to the public in 1966 and is now a general aviation facility, probably the finest on Long Island. It is also home to almost 400 private plane owners. Republic Airport relieves small plane traffic from larger airports in the New York area and serves as the base for many corporate aircraft.

Islip-MacArthur was established in 1942 as a "Defense Landing Area" by the federal government. In 1945, Sperry moved their flight operations there and developed remote-controlled aircraft. At the end of 1945 the Town of Islip took the airport over and by the early 1960s airline service began and a new control tower was constructed. In the 1960s the FAA built the New York Air Route Traffic Control Center, one of the busiest control routing centers in the country. Since then a new terminal and restaurant have been built and the runways extended. MacArthur has become a major airline feeder center, often with heavy jet traffic. It is also home to corporations installing new interiors and electronics in business jets. MacArthur has expanded to the point where it is the third busiest airport in New York State.

Small Aviation Manufacturers on Long Island

Smaller aviation-related manufacturers continued to thrive on Long Island in the 1950s. In the late 1950s, Sperry developed remote-control jet aircraft at MacArthur Airport. They also continued to build radar and bombing systems, and radar gunsights. Sperry built the advanced gyroscope and guidance system for the experimental X-15 rocket plane. Several small, new aerospace manufacturers were also established on Long Island in the postwar period. In 1950, the Gyrodyne Company of St. James produced its first helicopter—the Helidyne—which consisted of a rotary wing aircraft with additional conventional propellers for high-speed flight. Gyrodyne introduced its first coaxial helicopter, the Model 2C, in 1952. This type of helicopter, with counter-rotating main rotors, produces no torque and thus does not need a tail rotor. By far, Gyrodyne's most successful product was the QH-50 unmanned antisubmarine helicopter. The DASH (Drone Anti-Submarine Helicopter) was first produced in 1958 and continued in fleet service until 1972. The DASHes, carrying torpedoes, were remotely controlled from Naval destroyers. More than 650 were built in several versions. Gyrodyne also developed a unique hovercraft and the XRON one-man assault helicopter. Due to operational and financial problems, however, Gyrodyne was forced into bankruptcy in 1973.

Another helicopter manufacturer was established on Long Island in 1952 when the Convertawings Corporation of Amityville went into operation. Convertawings developed an experimental quadrotor (4 rotors) helicopter at Zahn's Airport, Amityville, which was intended to be the prototype for larger commercial versions. The Quadrotor flew many times in the 1950s, but no orders were forthcoming and the prototype was chopped up and buried. It was excavated and restored by the Cradle of Aviation Museum.[1]

One of Long Island's only missile manufacturers was

XRON–1 Rotorcycle, one of several tyes of
small helicopters built by Gyrodyne in the 1960s.

established in the early 1960s, when the Maxson Corporation of
Great River began to produce Bullpup missiles. The Bullpup was
an accurate and reliable air-to-surface missile with a two-mile
range. Flare-tracked and capable of achieving Mach 2 (twice the
speed of sound) speeds, the Bullpup missile was extensively used
in Vietnam for tactical use against surface targets requiring
accurate delivery. In fact, the vital Doumer Bridge north of Hanoi
was felled by a single Bullpup missile fired from an F-105. Maxson
also produced an expendable radio-controlled target missile
capable of flying at high altitudes and supersonic speeds. Due to
the lack of a need for air-to-surface missiles after the Vietnam War,
Maxson ceased operation in 1976.

The Continued Growth of Republic and Grumman

In the postwar period, the transition from propeller-driven to
jet-powered aircraft saved Republic as they had the foresight to
begin developmental work on a new jet fighter, the F-84
Thunderjet, in 1944. The F-84 quickly set several speed records
and the Air Force began to order large quantities in 1946. By 1947,

all Seabee and Rainbow work was halted and the gap was filled with F-84 orders. Cold War era rearmament led to even greater sales as newer, faster swept-wing versions of the F-84 were developed in the late 1940s and early 1950s and these were purchased in quantity by the Air Force as well as several NATO Allies. During the Korean War, 900 F-84s saw combat and some 250 were lost in action. Used mainly to attack ground targets, F-84s established a 7:1 kill ratio over Soviet jet MIGs during the war.

Republic won a contract in 1952 for a new fighter/bomber for the Air Force, the F-105 Thunderchief. By 1952, employment rose to 22,000, making Republic the largest employer on Long Island. Now there were three models of the F-84 in production and work began on the F-105. In the late 1940s and early 1950s, Republic was also working on two advanced experimental fighters, the XF-91 and the XF-103. The XF-91, of which only two were built, was the first dual mode (jet/rocket) fighter and the first aircraft having inversely tapered wings. The XF-103 was a highly advanced Mach 3 supersonic interceptor equipped with a dual mode (turbojet/

F-105D Thunderchief bombers under construction at
Republic's Farmingdale plant in the late 1950s.

ramjet) engine. Designed for high-speed, high-altitude interception, the first aircraft was under construction when the contract
was cancelled. It would have been the world's most advanced
aircraft.

The F-105 Thunderchief made its debut in 1955. It was, and
still is, the largest single engine, single-seat aircraft ever built. The
F-105 was designed for the high-speed delivery of nuclear
weapons at low altitude, combined with an air-to-air capability. In
1959, an F-105B set the world speed record of 1,216 mph at
Edwards Air Force Base in Project Fastwind. Used in Vietnam as a
tactical bomber, a role for which it was not designed, the F-105
was initially unsuccessful. Later in the war, F-105s were used for
Wild Weasel missions—to destroy enemy missile sites and in this
capacity they were very successful. Production continued on the
F-105 until 1964, by which time over 800 had been built. In
Vietnam 400 F-105s were lost. At the end of 1964, production had
ground to a halt at Republic. The F-105 fell victim to then
Secretary of Defense McNamara's concept of "commonality" of
service aircraft and was cancelled.

Republic then lacked any major airframe contract to pick up
the slack, and it was losing money on its major subcontract—
fabrication of the aft fuselage for the McDonnell F-4 fighter.
Employment dropped to 8,000 and the future looked bleak. Then,
in 1965, the Fairchild Corporation of Hagerstown, Maryland
purchased the operating assets of Republic Aviation and Republic
became a division of Fairchild. This was not a hostile takeover, as
Fairchild apparently hoped to revive the failing concern. Without
the Fairchild takeover, Republic probably would have ceased all
operations in 1965.

Republic won two large subcontracts in the late 1960s, to
build the aft fuselage and tail for the SST, and the wing control
surfaces for the Boeing 747. Republic invested $3 million on the
SST program and put up a new building for production, but the
program was terminated by Congress in 1971. The 747 program,
however, did represent a long-term profitable contract, and
production continued for 20 years until 1987 when all operations
ceased.

The years 1968–69 marked a turning point in the history of
the corporation. With no new aircraft production going on, the
engineering staff spent that time formulating detailed proposals to

build the newest Air Force Air Superiority fighter, the F-15. This was clearly going to be the Air Force's last new fighter contract for a long time to come. In early 1969, Republic was buoyed by their selection as one of three finalists for the project. However, in late 1969, McDonnell-Douglas, in a highly controversial and politicized decision, was selected to build the F-15. Had Republic won this contract, without doubt they would still be building them today. One of the major reasons Republic probably lost the F-15 contract was that weeks before the F-15 decision was announced, Grumman won the contract to build the Air Superiority F-14 fighter for the Navy. For geopolitical reasons it is doubtful that the Pentagon would have awarded two such major aircraft contracts to corporations only nine miles apart.

Once Republic lost the F-15 contract, they concentrated their remaining engineering efforts on another upcoming Air Force aircraft contract, a new Close Air Support aircraft (aircraft designed for destroying ground targets on the battlefield). After intense competition, the Air Force selected Republic's A-10 as its new Close Air Support plane in January 1973. Republic's A-10 was a powerful, heavily armed aircraft and the first Air Force plane specifically designed for Close Air Support. The contract for 720 A-10s was to be worth $1.5 billion. The A-10 was designed for the accurate delivery of ordnance at low altitude and high speed. Equipped with missiles, bombs, and a 30mm cannon Gatling gun, it was intended to counter Soviet armor in Europe. It would be able to survive intense antiaircraft fire due to its armor plating, redundant systems, and separated engines. It is still deployed in Europe today.

By 1980, A-10 production reached a peak of 144 aircraft with the last one built in 1984. However, many at Republic saw ominous warnings during the A-10 program as they believed the absentee management, Fairchild, was more concerned with profits than about jobs on the island , particularly after Fairchild moved half the work on the A-10 to Maryland.

The year 1980 also saw the company become deeply involved in a new, intensive competition for a follow-on aircraft for their A-10, that of building a new trainer for the Air Force. In 1982, Republic won the seemingly lucrative $1.5 billion contract. Production of the expected 650 T-46 aircraft was to run through 1992. The company also expected to increase sales through

Fairchild-Republic T-46 in flight over Jones Beach, mid-1980s.

derivatives, such as a light-attack version and foreign military sales. Two prototype T-46s were to be built with full production beginning in 1984. However, by 1985, engineering and manufacturing start-up costs on the T-46 trainer escalated, and this necessitated the addition of $89 million in corporate reserves to the project. These write-offs resulted from schedule slippages, engineering changes, and unforeseen start-up costs. As Fairchild-Republic had a fixed-price contract, they were forced to cover all costs above the contract ceiling.

Congress appropriated funds for 33 T-46s in FY (Fiscal Year) 1986, but the Air Force never released the money and it made no requests for T-46s the next year because of budgetary constraints. With the end of the Reagan era defense buildup in sight, the Air Force determined that the T-46 was low on its list of priorities and it just couldn't afford the plane. When money is limited, the military inevitably prefers new weapons systems to new trainers. After the Air Force made no request for T-46s in FY 1987, Congress cut $321 million from the Department of Defense budget for T-46s in FY 1987, thus delivering a lethal blow to the project.

In spite of a successful flight test program, both the Air Force and Fairchild decided not to proceed with the program, for purely fiscal reasons. In March 1987, Fairchild and the Air Force mutually agreed to terminate the existing contract for the T-46 and all production work was stopped immediately in order to avoid future losses. In all, Fairchild lost $120 million on the T-46 program; only four planes were built.

As no new business was coming in, Fairchild felt it necessary in 1987 to wind down operations at the Long Island plant, and dispose of it entirely in 1988. With contraction in the military aircraft industry and expected limitations on new programs, Fairchild could not see near or long-term opportunities for Republic as a military airframe builder. The remaining 3,500 employees were laid off as Fairchild decided to get out of aircraft production entirely. In 1988, the site of the Republic Aviation Corporation was sold, slated to become a shopping mall. An era was over after 26,173 aircraft had been built.

The major reason why Republic failed was they they failed to successfully diversify out of the military aircraft market. In today's tight defense budget climate, it is impossible for a company to survive solely as a military airframe producer. Republic could survive only as long as they could keep at least one major aircraft contract going. In retrospect, it couldn't have lasted forever.[2]

Grumman on the other hand, still builds a variety of aircraft and continues to thrive in the same tight defense budget climate. In the postwar period, Grumman recognized the need for a special mission aircraft, and created the AF-2 Guardian series of antisubmarine hunter-killer teams, with electronic search and detection systems. This was the first of the Navy's electronic aircraft, although comparatively few were built. This late 1940s aircraft successfully established Grumman's entry into electronics systems for aircraft which is still a Grumman specialty today.

Grumman produced its first jet fighter, the F9F Panther, by 1947. Successfully entering the jet age at its inception, the small, sleek F9F became the first carrier-based jet to enter combat in Korea. A follow-up variation, the Cougar, was the Navy's first swept-wing aircraft (wings angled back for greater speed). During the Cold War and Korean War rearmament programs, 3,370 Panthers and Cougars were built. The F9F saw action as a fighter/bomber in Korea, attacking enemy bridges, dams, and factories. It was a Grumman F9F Cougar that Lt. Commander F. Brady flew in April 1954 when he made the first transcontinental flight of under four hours. Brady flew from San Diego to Floyd Bennett Field, refueling once over Kansas. Transcontinental speed records were thus set on Long Island by a Wright biplane in 1911 and a Grumman F9F in 1954.

By 1952, Grumman developed the S-2 series of aircraft, combining the capabilities of the Guardian hunter-killer team into a single aircraft. The S-2 Tracker carried all the detection equipment and armament necessary to perform the anti-submarine warfare mission; 1,167 were built, most being heavily modified over a long flying career. Another modification developed in 1958 became the "eyes of the Fleet." The WF-2 Tracer, carrying a huge radome (plastic dome housing radar antenna) on its back, could warn a task force of potential aircraft, ship, or missile threats and direct interception by carrier planes. It continued Grumman's strong entry into avionics (aircraft electronics) and was the forerunner of today's E-2C Hawkeye.

In the early 1950s, Grumman also introduced its first "swing-wing" aircraft the XF10F-1 Jaguar. Although it pioneered the advanced swing-wing design (wings can be adjusted forward or back for various speed ranges), the XF10F-1 exhibited engine and control problems and none were ordered by the Navy. However, pioneering work on the XF10F-1 later helped Grumman win the F-111B and F-14 contracts. Its follow-up design, the F-11 Tiger introduced another new shape to high performance aircraft design, the "Coke bottle" fuselage that reduced drag at high speeds. The F-11 was the Navy's first supersonic aircraft, yet only 200 were produced, in part due to the short operational range of the aircraft.

In the mid 1950s, Grumman management proved its acumen by identifying the need for a low-cost, low maintenance crop duster to replace the government surplus trainers crudely adapted for spraying. Grumman's Ag-Cat was built for strength, maneuverability, and simplicity. Today it is flown worldwide in greater numbers than any other agricultural aircraft ever built. In the same period Grumman also recognized that there would soon be a need for a new executive transport to replace the hundreds of old DC-3s then in use. In 1958 Grumman entered the corporate transport aircraft field with its ten-passenger Gulfstream I. Two hundred were sold to corporations, government agencies, and foreign customers before it was succeeded in the late 1960s by the jet Gulfstream II. Grumman's successful entry into electronic aircraft continued when in 1959 they sold their first aircraft to the Army, the OV-1 Mohawk electronic surveillance aircraft. A twin-engine turboprop, it became the "airborne eyes" of Army field

Courtesy Grumman Corporation

Grumman E-2C Hawkeye, an early warning aircraft
deployed with the naval carrier fleet.

commanders in Vietnam and remains in operation today.

By 1960 two of the most successful aircraft in Grumman
history, the A-6A Intruder and the E-2A Hawkeye first flew. Both
of them, in modified form, remain in production today. The A-6, a
high-speed attack aircraft able to carry a large ordnance load, was
the Navy's main bomber in Vietnam. It was the first all-weather
attack aircraft with a computer-controlled attack system. Newer
versions of it are still being built today, 30 years after it first flew.
The E-2 was the first aircraft specifically designed for Airborne
Early Warning. It is able to track 600 targets at once and direct
their interdiction. The Hawkeyes, with their large radomes on
their backs have become a familiar sight to Long Islanders.

In 1969, (while Republic was fighting to win the F-15),
Grumman won the contract to build the Navy's newest Air
Superiority Fighter. After 14 years, Grumman was back in the
fighter business. Today's swing-wing F-14 flies at more than twice
the speed of sound, carries the most potent combination of
weapons of any fighter in the air, and can adjust its wings
automatically in flight to the best configuration for speed, attitude,
and altitude. The Grumman F-14 Tomcat can track 24 targets at
once up to 200 miles away and can attack 6 at once. To date, over
600 F-14s have been built.

By the early 1980s Grumman continued to develop a

Grumman F-14 Tomcat Navy fighter
with wings in fully swept position.

complete tactical Air Force. The advanced airborne early warning
E-2C Hawkeyes were produced for the Navy as well as for several
foreign governments. The A-6 attack bomber is still in production,
after 600 have been built. The A-6 was also used to develop the
EA-6B Prowler, a tactical jamming plane which contains the most
advanced electronic counter-measure equipment ever fitted to a
tactical aircraft. The EA-6B's electronic systems in turn were
modified to win Grumman a major contract to produce an Air
Force tactical jamming plane, the EF-111. Thus Grumman is now
producing on both sides of the electronics warfare game—they
manufacture both radar surveillance aircraft and radar jamming
aircraft. Grumman has also won several contracts to upgrade the
electronics on older aircraft, ranging from A-4 Skyhawks to
Chinese MIGs. In the late 1980s, aircraft electronics accounted for
one-third of all Grumman's business.

Grumman's newest aircraft design, the X-29 was built with a
1981 $80 million award to develop, build, and flight test two of
these radically designed experimental aircraft. This unique
aircraft featured forward swept wings (wings angled forward
instead of back) for greater maneuverability and low speed
handling, as well as a number of state-of-the-art technologies
including computerized flight controls and composite construction.
Both aircraft have undergone successful flight-test programs.

In the late 1980s, Grumman was expanding into the area of military space, defense electronics, and construction of trucks, but not in its traditional business of building aircraft. Their future role as a prime builder of military combat planes is uncertain. Their five current aircraft programs are aging and few new ones are on the horizon. In fact there is some question if F-14 production will extend beyond 1991. Grumman has successfully won the JSTARS (Joint Surveillance Target Attack Radar System) contract for the Army and Air Force, and they hope to build ten under a $4 billion contract. This program did not get much publicity, but it is almost as big and profitable as the F-14 program. In 1987 Grumman built 43 aircraft, 13,000 postal trucks, and 19,000 boats. Aerospace still accounts for 75 percent of their total sales. To date, Grumman has built over 33,000 aircraft. Thus Grumman is also rediscovering its basic strengths as a high quality electronics merchant. They are indeed looking beyond the mid-1990s when their current aircraft programs will most likely be phased out. Increasingly, Grumman will be making and integrating electronics systems and installing them in planes, possibly their own, but more likely those of other companies. Since today's electronics are far more profitable than building the whole plane, Grumman is evolving from a company that made aircraft, into a company that put electronics into them. And when defense money is tight, the Pentagon tends to improve existing systems such as aircraft, rather than buying new ones. Simply put, that means more electronics.

Today Grumman is simultaneously producing several types of aircraft as well as many other products, unlike Republic which consistently relied on one major program to support its whole operation. It is unlikely that all of Grumman's projects would be terminated at once. Fortunately for Long Island, Grumman is simply too diversified to meet the same ignominious end as Republic.[3]

Boeing 747 at Kennedy Airport, one of many types of modern airliners seen in the skies daily over Long Island.

Contemporary Aviation on Long Island

Today, two of the largest and busiest airports in the United States remain on Long Island, LaGuardia and Kennedy International. Flying has become so commonplace that by 1988 approximately one out of every eight people on earth has flown. To handle this heavy traffic in and out of New York, in the early 1980s the FAA constructed a new Transit Control (TraCon) center in Garden City, now one of the largest routing centers in the country. Nearby, in Westbury, Island Helicopters regularly flies businessmen and commuters from its busy heliport, so even to the present some form of aviation remains on the Hempstead Plains.

MacArthur, Republic, and the newer, smaller Brookhaven remain as heavily used general aviation and commuter airports. The skies over Long Island are still dotted with Cessnas and Pipers used for pleasure flying, flight instruction, and charter use. In 1988, there are also approximately 1,400 "general aviation"—private—aircraft based on Long Island. The sport of gliding is still practiced on Long Island at Brookhaven and Westhampton Beach airports and simple new planes called ultralights can also be seen. Many Long Island residents, usually members of the Experimental Aircraft Association, construct their own advanced aircraft of aluminum and fiberglass in their garages and basements. Bayport Aerodrome houses the Antique Airplane Club, so on good weekends many Wacos, Stinsons, and Stearmans of aviation's Golden Age still take to the air over Long Island. The fact that such aircraft are still flying serves to remind us how far we've come in such a fairly short time. Eighteen airports have existed in Nassau County since 1909. Grumman Airport is the last remaining one, but it is scheduled to close in 1990.

Grumman still remains Long Island's largest private employer, and it appears they will be building advanced aircraft until well into the forseeable future. There are also numerous smaller aerospace-related companies still manufacturing on Long Island. Sperry (re-named Unisys in 1987), EDO, Airborne Instrument Laboratory, and Hazeltine, for example, all construct highly advanced aircraft electronics systems. One of these small companies, Ames Industries of Bohemia, built a radical new aircraft in 1979 under a NASA contract. The Ames AD-1 was an experimental "scissor wing" jet, which successfully engaged in pioneering flight tests at Edwards Air Force Base. This was the first NASA research aircraft built on Long Island and it proved the pivoting wing concept, which can be applied to future supersonic airliners. Norden Systems in Melville also specializes in radar and navigation systems. Gull in Smithtown produces fuel and oil quantity gauging systems, as well as fuel flow systems and engine performance instrumentation.

Long Islanders see aircraft going over their heads daily, but today's Boeing 747s and SSTs do not turn nearly as many heads as did John Moisant's Bleriot in 1910. Aviation has shaped our lives to a degree greater than we can imagine. In all, more than 64,000 aircraft have been built on Long Island. That is a remarkable number in view of the fact that Long Island is not such a large area.

Probing the Final Frontier

Although Long Island has long been known as "the Cradle of American Aviation," it has also had a very long involvement with, and influence upon, the American Space Program. After hundreds of thousands of years of occupancy, and several thousand years of recorded history, humans at last left the planet Earth in the twentieth century and took the first hesitant steps on a world that was not their own. Long Islanders made these first steps possible.

Long Island's Involvement in the Early Days of Rocketry

Long Island's first involvement with spaceflight can be traced back to its earliest days and the pioneering rocketry experiments of Dr. Robert Goddard. In the early 1920s, while working in Massachusetts, Dr. Goddard developed the world's first liquid fuel rockets. Working largely on his own, he flew the world's first liquid fuel rocket in 1926, but a rather spectacular 1929 flight caused his work to be banned in Massachusetts. Charles Lindbergh read a report of this flight and, impressed with the possibilities of the rocket, brought it to the attention of his friends, philanthropists Daniel and Harry Guggenheim of Sands Point, Long Island.

Dr. Goddard and his wife came to Harry Guggenheim's home, Falaise, in 1929 to discuss the exciting future of rocketry and Goddard's need for major funding if he were to continue his research. Esther Goddard was enchanted by Guggenheim's manorial home which she described to her mother as "a French chateau effect, with peacocks, espaliered fruit trees, horses, dogs, a terrace overlooking the Sound . . . a fairyland."[1] (Falaise is now a Nassau County Museum.) Soon Dr. Goddard received a grant of $50,000 from Harry Guggenheim—through his private "Guggenheim Fund"—the first of several which allowed him to continue his research at a time when government sources thought of him as a "crackpot." With adequate funds, Goddard headed west to Roswell, New Mexico, where the climate and wide open spaces were perfect for his work. Today, a plaque next to the fireplace in Falaise notes the important connection between Dr. Goddard and the Guggenheims.

Goddard's rockets were almost completely custom-made. He ordered materials from hardware mail-order houses and his crew prowled through hardware stores, auto-parts outlets, and junkyards. When they found something that might do a particular job—a wristwatch, a length of piano wire, an automobile spark plug—they proceeded to use it to perform a function undreamed of by its manufacturers. A good deal of time had to be spent in the shop salvaging successful rockets that had been airborne. A successful flight meant jubilation and often, carrying home a pile of junk, all that remained after a crash landing. The smashed rockets could seldom be rebuilt, so Goddard designed and built the first rocket recovery system with parachutes to ensure softer landings.

The Guggenheim Fund grants financed Goddard's works until 1940. During that time he developed a reliable liquid fuel rocket engine, an efficient turbine fuel pump, and gyroscopic control with steering system. Given the tools and technology of the time, his achievements were remarkable. Goddard's rockets were the first man-made objects to exceed the speed of sound. Shortly after Goddard's death in 1945, German scientist Wernher Von Braun examined his rocketry patents and declared, "Goddard was ahead of us all." In all, Goddard received no fewer than 214 patents covering virtually every aspect of liquid-fuel rockets. Thanks to Long Island funding, Goddard is the man behind every rocket that flies.

Building Rockets and Missiles

As World War II was drawing to a close, it was clear that rockets and missiles would be the weapons of the future. To this end, Republic was awarded a contract in 1944 to build copies of the German V-1 Buzz Bomb, renamed the JB-2 Loon. Republic began delivering copies of a captured V-1 to the Army by January 1945, in just two months time. The JB-2s had a 150–mile range and were intended to be launched from submarines during the

Republic JB-2, America's first guided missile, 1945.

invasion of Japan. Although they were never used operationally, they were the first U.S. guided missiles and their construction gave the first practical experience in missile building.[2]

Grumman was awarded the contract to build the large Rigel ship-to-surface missile in 1946. Rigel was the earliest U.S. plan to develop a large submarine-launched shore-bombardment missile and, as such, was a predecessor of the Regalus, Polaris, and Poseidon missiles. Although Rigel itself did not become operational and was cancelled after Grumman worked on its development from 1946 to 1953, much was learned in the submarine and launching phase that was useful for the development of later missiles. Additionally, Rigel was Grumman's first missile project and led the company to expand its missile and spacecraft interests. The Rigel was also considered an early cruise missile and may have helped influence early strategic thinking along these lines. Thus Grumman's Rigel was the first successful U.S. "ramjet" missile, the first Mach 2 vehicle, and Grumman's first weapons system. Rigel had a solid-fuel first stage which boosted the missile to Mach 1 (the speed of sound), at which speed the ramjet kicked in and compressed air for the engine which boosted the missile to Mach 2. It had a 300–mile range at altitudes up to 50,000 feet. Thirteen Rigels were successfully launched from Point Mugu, California, between 1950 and 1953.[3] The sole survivor is now on display at the Cradle of Aviation Museum.

Republic continued its missile interests with the development of the scientific rocket, Terrapin, in 1956. Built to obtain data for use in the development of space vehicles, Terrapin was a joint project between Republic and the University of Maryland. An extremely lightweight vehicle, it carried an instrument package weighing six pounds. It was a two-stage solid propellent rocket 15 feet long. Designed for cosmic ray studies and upper-air temperature research, Terrapin raced 80 miles into space at 3,800 miles per hour on its initial firing. The intent behind Terrapin was to make an inexpensive rocket that could be handled, serviced, and launched by only a few people. It was the only Long Island built scientific research rocket.

Military rockets were also built on Long Island in the 1950s, at the Fairchild Guided Missiles Division in Wyandanch. The two major rockets the company produced, the Lark and Petrel, were for the U.S. Navy. The Lark was an early subsonic Naval missile whose contract originated in 1945. It was in quantity production by 1952, being employed both as a launching-crew training missile and as a surface-to-air flight test vehicle to prove a Fairchild-developed target homing system. The Lark was over 14 feet long, employed two solid-fuel booster rockets, and flew successfully over 100 times. The Petrel, operational in 1956, was a revolutionary new air-launched missile for use against submarines and surface ships. It was 24 feet long, had a 20–mile range, and carried a torpedo-type payload. It was the most complex U.S. Navy missile to date and featured an on-board computer that tracked targets on its own.

Sputnik I and the U.S. Race to Catch Up

On October 4, 1957, the United States was stunned by the launch of the Soviet *Sputnik I*, the world's first artificial satellite. The next day the *New York Times'* front page reported that the new satellite's signals were first detected by an RCA communications station at Riverhead, Long Island. Reacting to this alarming development, the Eisenhower administration responded by creating the National Aeronautics and Space Administration

(NASA) and initiating Project Mercury for the first men in space. Grumman was one of eight companies that competed for the contract to build the Mercury spacecraft and in late 1958, they were selected as one of the two finalists along with McDonnell. However, in January 1959, McDonnell was ultimately selected to build the spacecraft. As the then NASA administrator put it:

> The reason for choosing McDonnell over Grumman was the fact that Grumman was heavily loaded with Navy projects in the conceptual stage. It did not appear wise to select Grumman in view of its relatively tight manpower situation at the time, particularly since that situation might be reflected in a slow start on the capsule project regardless of priority. Moreover, serious disruption in scheduling Navy work might occur if the higher priority capsule project were awarded to Grumman.[4]

Nonetheless, Grumman had a great deal to do with the preliminary and final design of the spacecraft, as well as working out the orbital mechanics for the early missions. Moreover, the first two-manned Mercury missions were boosted into space on Redstone missiles which were controlled by on-board gyroscopes built by Sperry in their Long Island City plant.

Grumman established a Space Steering Group in 1958, whose task it was to target upcoming spaceflight contracts and develop procurement proposals. Their first successful spaceflight contract was won in 1960. The Orbiting Astronomical Observatory (OAO) was the most advanced satellite of the 1960s and America's first space telescope. The objective of the OAO program was to place a series of large unmanned satellites carrying astronomical equipment into the Earth's orbit where viewing is not obscured by the atmosphere. In all, Grumman built four OAO vehicles, two of which outperformed all expectations. The OAO-2 went into orbit in December 1968. Viewing instruments placed aboard this free flyer (orbits independently) opened a large portion of the electromagnetic spectrum to astronomical investigation and contributed greatly to our knowledge of galaxies, stars, and the solar system. Grumman's OAO-C3 achieved orbit in August 1972. This was the most sophisticated satellite of its time, and returned valuable scientific data continuously for the next ten years. During this long observational period, scientists were able to study the cosmos, including comets and novae, with a precision and clarity never before possible. Its unique on-board computer would probably still be processing and transmitting data if the experiments had not been terminated for economic reasons by the government in February 1982.[5]

Grumman won another spaceflight contract in 1961, this time for constructing nine canisters to launch the Echo Communications satellites. *Echo II,* first launched into orbit in January 1964, was the forerunner of today's widely used commercial communications satellites. The program involved launching a series of balloons into orbit to serve as a passive reflecting medium for relaying straight-line radio signals from one remote part of the Earth to another. Grumman's job was to produce the cannisters that housed the balloons into orbit as well as the adapters that mated the cannisters to the Atlas rocket.

Meanwhile in Farmingdale, Republic too was continuing their spaceflight work. In 1960, Republic was awarded the first NASA contract ever for an experimental Lunar Exploration Spacesuit. Although unwieldy, cylindrical in shape with tripod legs, use of the spacesuit gathered important information on how men performed in a spacesuit in a simulated lunar environment. Later in the 1960s, the follow-up program to Project Mercury was the two-man spacecraft Project Germini. Project Gemini was to be extended with the Air Force's Manned Orbiting Laboratory (MOL) program which was to be a primitive space station. Republic was contracted to build the living and laboratory quarters for this proposed space station; however, the project was terminated by Congress in 1968. In the early 1960s, Republic received a contract to develop preliminary studies of a three-man spacecraft designed for a 14–day lunar orbit mission. This project was ultimately developed by Rockwell as the Project Apollo Command Module. In 1961, Republic was awarded another contract to develop a pinch-plasma rocket engine. This small battery-powered engine used inert gases for fuel. These engines were used on one satellite, the LES-6 flown in the mid 1960s.

Republic won a very important contract in 1962 to develop the Project FIRE Spacecraft. Project FIRE was a NASA program designed to obtain research data during atmospheric re-entry at extremely high velocities. Republic built two miniature 200–pound Apollo Command Modules. The basis of the program was to test the Apollo heat shield and stability of the spacecraft at Lunar return speeds prior to building the actual spacecraft. During two successful flights, in 1964 and 1965, FIRE spacecraft were launched on Atlas missiles and tested total heating, radiative heating, radio signal communication, stability, and materials behavior during re-entry. At an altitude of 150 miles, during downward trajectory of the spacecraft, a second rocket attached to the vehicle was fired to supply the thrust required to reach the 25,000 mph lunar return velocity.[6]

In 1964, Republic began development of their first satellite, the Advanced Orbiting Solar Observatory (AOSO). The AOSO was designed to study solar phenomena and its complex interactions with the geophysical and space environments. This included such things as solar flares—high energy radiation emitted from the sun—which are sufficiently intense to cause a radiation hazard to spacecraft. The 1,500–pound AOSO carried a 250–pound scientific payload and was placed in a 300–mile polar orbit so it could observe the sun without interruption for many months. The AOSO conducted the first detailed investigation of sunspots and solar flares, which aided in their future prediction.

Space Race to the Moon

Wanting to build on its success with its earlier space programs, Grumman continued to seek new spaceflight contracts. In May 1961, President Kennedy announced his plans for landing a man on the Moon by the end of the decade. The Space Race had begun. NASA had abandoned the idea of using a single spacecraft for the Moon trip and were debating the merits of several alternative missions. Grumman favored the Lunar Orbit Rendezvous approach, which permitted specialization of vehicles, and thus they concentrated on designing a lunar landing vehicle that would carry astronauts from the spacecraft orbiting above the lunar surface down to the Moon and back.

Based on studies submitted to NASA during the course of the debate, Grumman was invited to bid for the Lunar Module contract along with ten other aerospace companies (including Republic). In November 1962, NASA Administrator James Webb personally announced that Grumman had won the competition. Thus Grumman was to build the Project Apollo Lunar Module, undoubtedly the most historic vehicle ever built on Long Island. It was also the first vehicle designed to take men from one world to another.

From the outset, construction of the Lunar Module (LM) posed a set of unique engineering problems. Designed solely for the one-sixth gravity and vacuum of the Moon, it had to be a new type of vehicle performing a new type of role. Fortunately the LM could take on any shape, for it needed to possess no aerodynamic requirements. Unlike previous, or subsequent spacecraft, it operated solely outside the Earth's atmosphere.

Functionally, the LM had to satisfy five major criteria: (1) small enough to stow inside the Saturn V rocket and light enough to be boosted into orbit; (2) self-propelled and able to maneuver with precision in space; (3) a life-support system for astronauts operating in a hostile environment; (4) a communications center, maintaining contact with the orbiting Apollo spacecraft as well as ground stations on Earth; (5) double as a lifeboat in the event of a breakdown in one of the other Apollo Modules. This last provision was added as an afterthought by Grumman engineers. Weight was extremely critical on the LM, the heavier it was the more fuel it would burn looking for a safe place to land on the Moon. In fact, the pressure shell on the LM was 2/1000 of an inch thick, the same as two sheets of paper. The LM was a two-stage vehicle. The descent stage, having its own engine, served as the launch pad for the ascent stage which lifted the two astronauts off the Moon. This lightened the vehicle even further, but also brought in the problem of having fail-safe disconnects.

The design set forth in Grumman's winning proposal evolved through several configurations over the next few years and kept on evolving through each successive mission. As the complexity of the task increased, so did the number of people working on it. At the peak of activity, 9,000 Grumman employees were assigned to the program. During the early years of the program, the LM underwent considerable design change. The number of landing legs was reduced from five fixed, to four folding legs. The legs were widely spaced so the LM couldn't easily tip over. Large footpads were also added to the legs so the LM wouldn't sink into deep Lunar dust, if there was any. A second circular docking hatch was replaced with a larger, lighter square hatch to save weight and make it easier for the astronauts to get in

Courtesy Grumman Corporation

Lunar Module under construction
in Grumman's "Clean Room."

and out. A ladder was added down the front leg, instead of a knotted rope. An aluminized mylar, gold-colored foil was added to the exterior as a thermal insulation blanket. All of the LMs were built under intense pressure to beat the Soviets and land on the Moon before the end of the decade. This resulted in most Grumman employees working twelve-hour days, seven days a week for extended periods of time. Other Long Island companies were also involved in the LM program, including Republic which built the docking simulator, and EDO of College Point which built the landing leg probes.

As work progressed on the LM, Grumman engineers had to resolve many unusual technical questions such as spacecraft vulnerability to radiation, thermal control of the internal environment, and, most challenging of all, equipping a manned spacecraft to operate in near vacuum with extreme temperature variations and low gravity. Unlike aircraft, the LMs were not produced on an assembly line. Each one was handmade, one at a time, like a fine violin. Each intricate part was hand-milled from solid stock. In all, it took two and one-half years to build each vehicle.[7]

The low-gravity lunar environment had some positive impact on the design too. The LM required less lift-off and maneuvering power, a very light structural frame, and only a thin outer skin. By Earth standards, it seemed to be a flimsy contraption. The ladder on which the astronauts descended to the Moon's surface would have crumpled under a man's weight on Earth. The LM's legs each contained a simple aluminum honeycomb shock absorber to absorb the impact of landing since hydraulic systems would have been too heavy and complicated. The LM's propulsion system was simple and reliable. It used hypergolic propellants—two chemicals that exploded on contact so no igniter was needed.

One very high priority in the LM's development was vehicle safety and reliability. To meet this high standard, Grumman built redundancy, where possible, into all areas of LM performance. If a component or system failed anywhere, a backup was ready to take over its function. The guidance computer, for example, had three redundant circuits. In an emergency, the astronauts could override the computer and take manual control of the vehicle. This actually happened on the first lunar landing, when Neil Armstrong noticed that the LM was heading for a boulder field and took control from the computer, landing the spacecraft safely in a clear area. In all the lunar missions there was never a failure of any major LM component.

During the course of the Apollo Program, Grumman produced twelve operational LMs as well as ten test modules and two simulators. The first two LMs were designed for unmanned orbital flight only; the first, launched in January 1968, worked so well the second was never used. In March 1969, the next LM was flown in the first Apollo-manned Earth orbital trial, Apollo 9, which achieved 151 revolutions of the Earth in just under ten days. Two months later, in May, the fourth LM was launched on the Apollo 10 flight which made 31 lunar revolutions during which astronauts flew the LM down to within 47,000 feet of the Moon's surface. The LM's descent stage was successfully jettisoned on one lunar orbit and the ascent stage returned its crew to the orbiting Command Module. Everything was ready for the long-awaited moonshot.

On July 20, 1969, *Apollo 11*—LM-5 Eagle—landed astronauts Neil Armstrong and Buzz Aldrin on the Moon's "Sea of Tranquility." In the words of Armstrong it was, "One small step for man, one giant leap for mankind." President Kennedy's goal had been accomplished.[8] With variations in mission objective, payload, and landing site, this historic event was to be repeated five more times, the last occurring in December 1972. *Apollo 12* landed on the "Ocean of Storms" just 600 feet from its target, an old Surveyor spacecraft. This was a remarkable feat of navigation when one considers they had to travel over 250,000 miles to get there.

The *Apollo 13* LM *Aquarius* didn't land on the Moon, but it played a pivotal role in the legendary rescue that bears testimony to Grumman's creative imagination and engineering ingenuity. In April 1970, on the outward bound leg of the mission, an oxygen tank in the Service Module exploded, completely wiping out the Command Module's life support, fuel, and electrical systems. In one instant, a seemingly routine mission turned into an unprecedented technological challenge for hundreds of NASA and Grumman specialists on the ground and a life-threatening drama for the astronauts on board.

Fortunately, *Apollo 13* was outward bound, rather than returning from the Moon, because the LM, still docked to the Command Module, had not yet used any of its propulsion, power, or life-support systems. The only option for survival was the LM. At this point it was to act out the worst-case scenario anticipated by its Grumman designers—playing the role of lifeboat and tugboat for the damaged spacecraft and its crew.

Over the next few days it was touch and go for the *Apollo 13* mission. With the Command Module powered down to conserve energy for the final descent to Earth, the crew retreated to the LM, depending on it alone for propulsion to keep the spacecraft on course and for food, air, and water to keep them alive during the long wait for splashdown. On the ground the world was stunned by the events taking place aboard *Apollo 13*. Hundreds of NASA and Grumman personnel worked around the clock, frantically trying to come up with answers to hundreds of perplexing questions, ingeniously inventing ways of conserving the spacecraft's dwindling supplies of energy and life-sustaining consumables.

Three times during the tense journey homeward, engine burns from the LM propulsion system kept the damaged spacecraft on course. On the morning of April 17, four days after the explosion, the *Apollo 13* crew jettisoned the dead Service Module. They then powered up the Command Module, transferring energy from the LM's batteries, and with "Farewell Aquarius . . . we thank you," jettisoned the LM and safely reentered the Earth's atmosphere.[9]

Grumman's Lunar Modules performed nearly flawlessly on the last four Apollo missions. *Apollo 14* landed at Fra Mauro, on the rim of a giant crater. *Apollo 15* was the first of three full-fledged science missions and and was the first to carry a Lunar Roving Vehicle. It landed at Hadley Rille near a huge canyon. *Apollo 16* set down at Descartes crater which they thought might be volcanic but wasn't. Finally in December 1972, *Apollo 17* landed at the bottom of the Taurus-Littrow Valley as the LM flew between mountains thousands of feet high. Today, an original Grumman Apollo Lunar Module can be seen at the Cradle of Aviation Museum in Garden City.

Project Apollo gave us an incredible amount of new scientific knowledge. Furthermore, the commercial and technological spin-offs generated by Apollo are still paying off. Apollo was also of tremendous inspirational value and it generated a great deal of national pride. In all, 12 astronauts left their bootprints in the lunar dust, and they brought home nearly a thousand pounds of rocks that proved to be up to 4.6 billion years old. But Apollo also brought home something less tangible, though no less important: a new appreciation for the beauty and fragility of "spaceship Earth" as it hurtles through the heavens. For the first time we saw our own blue planet through the traveller's eye and camera—"a beautiful oasis in the vastness of space." In the entire Solar System, billions of miles across, only Earth, so far as we know, sustains the magnificent variety of life that we so casually accept. Only by thoroughly understanding our planet, can we hope to learn how to use its limited resources wisely and to preserve for future generations our island in space. And that is what the true significance of Project Apollo was.

Concurrently with building the Lunar Module, Grumman was also developing two types of Lunar Roving Vehicles (LRV). Beginning in 1961, Grumman developed "Molab"—a large Mobile Lunar Laboratory in which two astronauts could explore hundreds of miles in a shirtsleeve environment. Molab was built with Grumman funds, but was used to investigate, under a NASA contract, the driving characteristics of a Lunar Roving Vehicle over a simulated lunar surface. For this purpose Grumman built a two-acre simulated lunar surface at their Calverton plant. The two-section, four-wheeled Molab was pressurized, had controls, work areas, seats, beds and communications system. Although never produced for Lunar use, Molab gathered the first information on how vehicles perform over a simulated lunar surface. Later in the 1960s, Grumman competed with Boeing to build the small Lunar Roving Vehicles that would be carried on the final three Apollo missions. Grumman's proposal was for a two-section vehicle that featured elastic, conoidal puncture-proof wheels, that afforded large "footprints" for weak-soil mobility. The LRV could be driven manned or remote-controlled from Earth. Although Grumman won a preliminary design contract from NASA, they ultimately lost the construction to Boeing. However, Grumman's LRV prototype was to enjoy a long and colorful career. Grumman was awarded an Army contract to test this same LRV in 1981 as a remote-controlled antitank weaponry platform. They were ultimately awarded a contract to develop "Robot Ranger" attack vehicles from it.

Long Island, the Space Shuttle, Space Station, and Beyond . . .

During the early 1960s, both Grumman and Republic were also involved in developing design studies for a small two or three man reusable spacecraft. Called "Dyna-Soar," for Dynamic Soaring Vehicle, the spacecraft was to be launched on an expendable Titan rocket. However, this prototype space shuttle never got beyond the mockup stage. By the mid 1960s it was cancelled in favor of the faster and cheaper Mercury/Gemini Space Programs.

In 1969, NASA initiated feasibility studies to build a large new type of reusable spacecraft—a space shuttle. Grumman immediately entered the design competition. Over the course of the next three years, Grumman developed several detailed design proposals that had a fundamental influence on the final design of the space shuttle orbiter. In order to bring down operational cost and for increased safety, Grumman's initial proposals centered around a two-stage, fully reusable vehicle. This would feature a straight-wing Grumman orbiter, riding atop a manned flyback Boeing booster which would separate from the orbiter at 40 miles altitude. Due to high development costs, this was then scaled back to the orbiter riding atop an expendable or reusable Saturn V rocket first stage. At the same time, Grumman was the first company to develop the idea of an external fuel tank. This resulted in a smaller, cheaper, and simpler orbiter. When a liquid fuel booster proved too expensive to develop, given current cost constraints, Grumman and others were forced to use the idea of solid fuel boosters. Grumman's first ideas featured the solid rocket boosters mounted in tandem, that is, below the external fuel tank. The current shuttle design has the boosters in parallel, that is, alongside the external fuel tank. If a *Challenger*-type burn-through had occurred in Grumman's early design, the errant flame could not have impinged on the external fuel tank. Grumman's ultimate design proposal was generally similar to today's space shuttle except that it had maneuvering thrusters in the wing tips, a docking port in the nose, and deployable jet engines for a go-around capability. Grumman was one of the two finalists, but in 1972, Rockwell was awarded the contract to build the space shuttle orbiter. At the time, the Pentagon felt Grumman was too heavily engaged in producing the F-14 and couldn't take on the additional work.

Nonetheless, major portions of the space shuttle were built on Long Island. Republic unsuccessfully bid on contracts for the space shuttle tailcone, solid rocket boosters, and waste management system. During this period Republic was building the toilet (nicknamed "Astrojohn") for the Skylab Space Station which was operational in 1973–74. When the Skylab Space Station was initially launched, the combination micrometeoroid-heat shield was torn off, causing the temperatue of the interior to rise uncontrollably. Grumman swiftly designed a parasol shield that the astronauts could erect in space to cool the interior. Working around the clock, a team of engineers and machinists produced the rods for the heatshield and flew them to Houston for the

Courtesy Grumman Corporation

The huge wings of the Space Shuttle
nearing completion at Grumman in Bethpage.

astronauts to practice with. The astronauts, with Grumman's
heatshield, were launched shortly thereafter and they successfully
deployed the shield on Skylab. Thus Grumman played a key role
in saving the multibillion dollar skylab program.

Republic won the contract to build the vertical fin and
rudders for the shuttle. Six sets of the large fins and rudders were
built at Farmingdale between 1974 and 1983. The rudder can split
in the middle to operate as a speed brake upon landing.
Grumman built the massive sets of shuttle wings. This was a
major challenge since the wings had to accommodate both
aerodynamic and entry heating induced loads with no skin
buckling. Each delta-shaped wing is made of aluminum and
weighs about 7,000 pounds. It measures 30 feet wide by 70 feet
long and is nearly 6 feet thick. Six sets of Shuttle wings were built
in Bethpage between 1973 and 1984. Upon completion they were

trucked to Oyster Bay, and from there barged through the Panama Canal and mated to the shuttle fuselage in California.

Many other Long Island companies built smaller space shuttle components including: Sperry (now Unisys) which built Univac computers that monitored and controlled the space shuttle's flight as well as some of its instrumentation; IMC Magnetics which built the internal components for the space shuttle toilet; and Hazeltine which built the microwave landing system.

Long before the space shuttle was flown, NASA began training its pilots in a real airborne environment using three Grumman Gulfstream II aircraft, structurally modified and instrumented by Grumman specifically for this purpose. The Shuttle Trainer Aircraft (STA) were equipped with a shuttle-like cockpit, a special on-board computer, and other equipment to accurately simulate the shuttle's powerless approach and landing and other unique flight characteristics.

Another Grumman-built training device, in this case for astronauts performing satellite servicing tasks in space, is the ground-based Large Amplitude Space Simulator (LASS), located in Bethpage. LASS is the best available real-life dynamic simulator of the shuttle's 50–foot articulated mechanical arm that rises out of the shuttle cargo bay to perform such tasks as placing payloads into orbit or retrieving them from orbit for servicing. NASA has used LASS not only for training shuttle crews for satellite servicing tasks, but also for developing the tools they will use, such as the Grumman-built Manipulator Foot Restraint.

A satellite servicing aid, the Manipulator Foot Restraint (MFR, or "Cherry Picker"), is a highly maneuverable work platform for shuttle crew members performing in-orbit maintenance or servicing tasks. It attaches to the end of the robot arm and provides a sturdy work platform to which astronauts can secure themselves and their tools. In April 1984, the MFR was used in the orbital repair of the Solar Maximum (Solar Max) Satellite.

Through the 1980s two unmanned NASA deep space probes called Voyager sailed through the Solar System, gathering for the first time closeup photos and other scientific information of our neighboring planets in the Solar System. The head of the Voyager Imaging Team for several of these planetary flybys was Dr. Toby

Owen of the State University of New York at Stony Brook.

In 1984, NASA initiated a new series of design competitions for various elements of a permanently manned Space Station to be launched in the 1990s. The Space Station will be a permanent research and work center in orbit. It will be used to conduct research and experiments in such areas as medicine, astronomy, solar studies, materials processing, and Earth resources. It will also serve as a platform to repair satellites and a spacecraft assembly area for future manned and unmanned exploration of the Solar System. In 1987, Grumman won the Space Station Program Support Contract. This billion-dollar contract is to assist NASA by coordinating the overall integration and management of the Space Station Project, including evaluation and oversight of the four aerospace companies chosen to design and build the major components of that facility. Later in 1987, Grumman won a contract to build the interior of the Space Station Habitat Module. The Habitat Module is where the astronauts will eat, sleep, relax, exercise, and monitor functions of the Space Station. Grumman will be developing zero-gravity sleeping quarters, dining area, and bathroom including chairs, television sets, sleep restraints, and exercise devices.

Grumman is also developing support equipment for the Space Station. This includes the Orbital Maneuvering Vehicle (OMV), a small remote-controlled "free-flying" device that will be useful in repairing instruments and satellites in space. When a satellite has a problem, the OMV will fly from the Space Station to the Satellite and tow it back for repairs. Telerobotic equipment (robot equipment operated by remote control), controlled by an operator on the ground, or Space Station, would be used to work on the broken satellites. After repair, the OMV would transport it back to its operational location.

The Space Station's modules, experiments, and solar panels will all be attached to a skeletal trusswork keel structure. Development of this space trusswork (a series of interconnecting struts) is being led by Starnet of West Babylon. Starnet is currently pioneering the field of Astrotechtonics, that is, construction in space. For this purpose Starnet has developed a lightweight, easily assembled truss system, composed of aluminum nodes and composite struts. The backbone of the Space Station will be formed of a series of cubes of this truss, each cube measuring 16 square feet per side. The trusswork will be brought into orbit by the Space Shuttle and then be manually assembled by two or three astronauts working without tools, as the truss simply snaps together. This truss can also be used in space for reflector telescopes, communications arrays, Strategic Defense Initiative Platforms, and hangars for spacecraft repair and servicing.[10]

In 1989 there are about 90 astronauts in the U.S. Space Program. They fly science and research missions on the space shuttle, deploy satellites, and will be used to man the future Space Station. Of these 90 astronauts, five are originally from Long Island. They are: Mary Cleave of Great Neck, Jeff Hoffman of Brooklyn, Karol Bobko of Seaford, and Robert Gibson and James Weatherbee of Huntington. By 1990 all will have flown on the shuttle at least once and most of them several times.

An example of an interesting science experiment flown on the space shuttle occurred during its March 1989 flight. A Chromex plant experiment was conducted to understand the effect of spaceflight on plants. It provided data important to Space Station and Lunar/Mars Base closed-cycle life support systems. The objectives of the experiment were to assess the effects of spaceflight on root growth, plant chromosomes, and plant cell division. The test was sponsored by the State University of New York at Stony Brook.

One of the major projects taking place in the Space Program today is the development of the Strategic Defense Initiative (SDI). This proposed system is being developed as a defense against enemy nuclear missiles, and at least portions of it are expected to be deployed around the turn of the century. SDI is where the majority of spaceflight research and development money is being expended today, and it accounts for the major share of Grumman's space business. To date, Grumman has procured contracts in three major areas of the Strategic Defense Initiative. Their prime contract is to develop the Boost Surveillance and Tracking System (BSTS) Satellite. The BSTS is a highly advanced satellite that is designed to detect enemy missile launches, lock onto their flight, and relay this information to a weaponry system that will then destroy them. Grumman is also developing a Space Based Radar (SBR) which will be a large deployable radar system set up in space. The SBR will be used to detect low flying enemy bombers and cruise missiles and to discriminate between re-entry vehicles carrying warheads and harmless decoys. For this, Grumman has pioneered in developing technology for an extremely light antenna array that rolls out like a window shade. The one SDI weapons system that Grumman is developing is a Neutral Particle Beam (NPB). The NPB platform is designed to fire a beam of high-energy, electrically neutral, atomic particles near the speed of light. This beam, like a powerful lightning bolt, can be transferred in a fraction of a second over many thousands of miles to the subatomic structure of an enemy missile, destroying it from within. Grumman is working with Brookhaven National Laboratory to develop the NPB. Should the SDI program be fully funded (which is uncertain at this time) it would be the major new thrust in the Space Program on Long Island.

Brookhaven National Laboratory is also doing advanced work on several other spaceflight projects. They are developing a nuclear rocket engine that would power a proposed Orbital Transfer Vehicle (OTV). The unmanned OTV would move payloads and satellites from Low Earth Orbit to Geo-synchronous orbit, and back for repair if necessary. A nuclear rocket engine for the OTV would have an advantage in that it would require little fuel and could operate for a long time.

The most exciting development on the spaceflight horizon is the hypersonic National Aerospace Plane. This would be a large single-stage-to-orbit aircraft that would take off from a runway and fly directly into space. It would be powered by a "scramjet" engine that would be a dual mode jet/rocket engine. When this vehicle becomes a reality in the late 1990s, it will revolutionize spaceflight, making it both cheaper and safer. Pioneering research for this crucial program is being conducted by General Applied Science Laboratory (GASL) of Ronkonkoma. GASL is assisting in the development of both the airframe and and scramjet engine both through computer simulations and testing with precise models in their five wind tunnels. GASL is presently under contract to NASA, the Air Force, and several manufacturers to define aerodynamic and engine configurations for the National Aerospace Plane.

Perhaps the most visionary spaceflight project ever undertaken on Long Island is now taking place at Brookhaven National Laboratory. Scientists there are conducting advanced theoretical work in planning the design and logistics for an antimatter powered Interstellar Spacecraft. This large manned spacecraft would carry small amounts of antimatter which when combined with matter, explode with tremendous energy. Using such a system, scientists believe they can accelerate the craft to near-light speeds and thus reach the nearest Star Systems in five years time. They believe such a spacecraft can be built in about the year 2050.

Virtually every major U.S. Space Project, past, present, and future, has had or will have, outstanding contributions by Long Island and Long Islanders. Clearly, Long Island has had a long and colorful involvement in the history of aviation and spaceflight, and it seems we will continue to do so for well into the foreseeable future, of which we can all be proud.

The Brewster Company's F2A Buffalo, circa 1940.

Appendix

Aviation Manufacturers

This includes some of the more detailed and technical information on the companies. Firms are listed alphabetically. The date in parenthesis is when the company was founded on Long Island.

American Aeronautical Corporation (1928)

American Aeronautical in Port Washington built one large S-55 12–passenger, twin-hull monoplane flying boat, but no commercial orders were forthcoming. Their successful S-56 was a wooden-hulled, simple, easy-to-fly plane and one set a nonrefueled endurance record (22 hours) for amphibians in 1930. S-56s were also the first aircraft to be used by any police department, as the New York City Police kept two at Floyd Bennett Field. American Aeronautical went bankrupt in 1931.[1]

American Airplane & Engine Corporation (1931)

American Airplane & Engine in Farmingdale operated for less than two years. Their Pilgrim aircraft was a large single-engine monoplane that was intended for cargo hauling or other utility use.

Brewster (1932)

The Brewster Aeronautical Corporation's most famous plane was the F2A Buffalo. In 1938, the F2A won the Navy's "Fly Off" against Grumman's F4F and soon they had hundreds of orders. These aircraft were fairly slow and not very maneuverable, and they were withdrawn from U.S. Naval service after many were shot down at the Battle of Midway in 1942. However, exported Buffalos did remarkably well in Finnish service, fighting against the Russians during World War II. In fact, Buffalos established a 26:1 kill ratio over Soviet aircraft, the highest ratio of any Long

Island built plane. Brewster also produced 500 SB2A Buccaneer dive bombers, which were not successful, and 600 Vought Corsairs under license.[2]

Brunner-Winkle (1928)

Brunner-Winkle's Bird was a three-seat, open cockpit biplane powered by surplus OX-5 engines. Later models were powered by K-5 engines once the OX-5 supply was exhausted. Elinor Smith set an altitude record in a Bird and Charles Lindbergh taught his wife to fly on one. Several Brunner-Winkle Birds are still flying to this day.[3]

Burnelli (1912)

Vincent Burnelli was actively involved in aviation development on Long Island during the 1920s. Burnelli was an early advocate of the lifting body type of aircraft and he held that the more conventional tube-shaped fuselage was practically deadweight between the wings. Burnelli moved to Long Island in 1907. His first powered aircraft was a pusher reconnaissance biplane for the Air Sevice which was demonstrated at Hazelhurst Field. In 1921, Burnelli built the first of a new type of plane, the lifting body, in which the airfoil-shaped fuselage generated lift. Burnelli's RB-1, a twin-engine biplane, was built in Amityville and was flown from Roosevelt Field for several years. Burnelli's ideas may continue to have some impact on the development of aviation for well into the forseeable future.[4]

Columbia (1943)

Work began in 1944 on a successor to the Duck, the XJL amphibian. The XJL was a large 8–seat single-engine monoplane whose ancestry can be traced directly back to Grumman's Duck of the mid-1930s which Columbia had produced under a subcontract. Tested by the Navy in Maryland in 1948, the two XJLs were sold as surplus in 1949.

Cox-Klemin (1921)

Cox-Klemin began at College Point and moved to Baldwin in 1924. Though they produced only 16 aircraft, several were notable. The CK-2A training plane was of advanced construction with an all-steel welded fuselage. Cox-Klemin developed the CK-1 and CK-18 passenger amphibious aircraft, the XO-4 observation plane, the Nighthawk mailplane, as well as the XA-1, the first aircraft specifically designed as a flying ambulance.

Curtiss (1918)

After moving to Garden City in 1918, the Curtiss Company developed the Challenger, C-6 and D-12 Conqueror engines, and the Curtiss-Reed all-metal propeller. The D-12 was the most advanced aircraft engine of its day. The historic Curtiss-Reed design was the first one-piece all-metal propeller. Curtiss developed some of the best-known aircraft of the Golden Age on Long Island. These include such diverse types as the biplane Condor airliner/bomber, the Robin private aircraft, the Fledgling trainer, the Oriole sportplane, the Carrier Pidgeon mailplane, the Falcon observation plane, the Hawk fighter, and the R-3 racers. The fastest aircraft in the world, the R-3 racers won the 1922 and 1923 Schneider Trophy Race. Curtiss also developed the giant NC transatlantic flying boats, the Bleeker helicopter, the 18–T triplane fighter, the MF flying boat, and the Tanager which won the 1930 Guggenheim Safe Aircraft Competition.[5]

Dade (1930)

Dade was in operation until 1945.

EDO (1925)

Earl D. Osborne founded EDO to manufacture all-metal aircraft floats. Their first floats were installed on a Waco in 1926. The demand for aircraft floats expanded in the 1930s and EDO produced thousands, including those for such famous planes as Charles Lindbergh's Lockheed Sirius and Admiral Byrd's Curtiss Condor. EDO also built most of the original Seversky aircraft, the SEV-3. In 1944, EDO developed the XOSE Scout seaplane for the Navy, although only two were built before the contract was cancelled. It was the last American catapult-launched (shot from a ship) aircraft. The electronic equipment EDO manufactured in the late 1980s included missile launchers, bomb racks, mine countermeasures systems, and advanced antisubmarine warfare sonar systems.[6]

Fairchild (1925)

Fairchild's FC-1 was the first aircraft specifically designed for aerial photography. Admiral Byrd's Fairchild FC-2 was the first aircraft to fly over Antarctica and it extensively mapped parts of that little-known continent. His *Stars and Stripes* is presently in the collection of the National Air & Space Museum in Washington, D.C.[7]

General (1940)

General Aircraft of Queens made its first plane in 1941. The Skyfarer was an easy-to-fly civilian aircraft. General Aircraft closed in 1945.

Grumman (1930)

See the previous text for full information.

Ireland (1926)

The Ireland Aircraft Company at Roosevelt Field had backing by R.J. Reynolds, the tobacco heir. Between 1927 and 1929 they produced the Neptune, a five-place amphibian with an aluminum hull. In 1929 they developed the Privateer, a stable, rugged monoplane amphibian.[8]

LWF (1915)

The LWF Engineering Company pioneered moulded plywood aircraft construction (monocoque) in which the strength of the fuselage comes from the plywood shell. After moving to College Point in 1916, they built the first aircraft in which an American Liberty engine was installed. The Liberty was the first mass-produced military aircraft engine. LWF aircraft were known for their ruggedness of construction. LWF was kept in business through the war years by their construction of over 30 Curtiss HS2L flying boats under subcontract. One of the more interesting LWF planes was the massive Owl bomber which was the largest American aircraft in 1920. Today one LWF survives, a Model V, now in the National Technical Museum in Prague. It was used on the Eastern Front in World War I.[9]

Loening (1932)

The Loening Aeronautical Engineering Company of New York City which had been founded in 1923, was responsible for building a successful series of amphibious aircraft for the Army and Navy, beginning with the COA-1 in 1924. The Loening Aircraft Company was established in Mineola in 1932 after Grover Loening sold his large New York City concern.

Orenco (1917)

The Ordnance Engineering Company in Baldwin from 1917

to 1922 built the Model B, the first U.S. fighter design to benefit from wartime combat experience. Designed with French input along the lines of their Spad fighter, it was also the first fighter to have wing-mounted machine guns which anticipated later designs. Orenco's most successful aircraft was the Model D fighter, of which Curtiss built 50 in Garden City in 1919. Curtiss won the construction bid as, at the time, the original designer didn't have the production rights. The only surviving Orenco aircraft is a Model D, now in the Weeks Air Museum in Florida.

Ranger (1934)
Ranger was in operation until 1955.

Republic (1931)
See previous text for full information.

Sikorsky (1923)
Among Sikorsky's 65 aircraft produced on Long Island in the 1920s, first in Roosevelt and later College Point, was the S-35 in which Rene Fonck attempted to fly the Atlantic. Their most successful aircraft was the S-38 amphibian which was used by several airlines.[10]

Sperry (1917)
The Messingers Sperry produced in the 1920s were small, general-use planes powered by 64 hp three-cylinder Lawrance engines designed by Long Islander Charles Lawrance. In fact, Lawrence Sperry regularly flew a Messenger from the street in front of his Garden City home. He also landed one on the Capitol steps in Washington. In 1922, they produced the Sperry-Verville R-3 Racer, the first monoplane with retractable landing gear. A highly streamlined aircraft, the R-3 presaged fighters of the 1930s. This aircraft briefly held the world speed record. Sperry also built a triplane amphibian which was remarkably fast for its day.[11]

Vought (1920)
The Vought Corporation of Long Island City produced the VE-7 which, in 1922, was the first aircraft launched from an American aircraft carrier. By far their most successful airplane was the O2U Corsair, a two-seat, radically new observation/scout aircraft, which displayed performance equal to most single-seat fighters of its day.[12]

Notes

The Dawn of Flight, pages 11–14

1. Preston Bassett, "Aeronautics on Long Island." In *Long Island History*, ed. by Paul Bailey. (New York: Lewis Publishing, 1949), II:410.
2. New York State Division of Commerce, *New York State Writer's Project*, 1939, p. 11.
3. Tom Crouch, *A Dream of Wings*, (New York: W.W. Norton, 1981), p. 203.
4. Joshua Stoff, "America's First Powered Flights—Over Brooklyn!" *Long Island Forum* 48 (May 1985): 84.
5. E.E. Husting, "Augustus Herring, Pioneer Aviator," *National Soaring Museum Journal* 1 (Winter 1976): 3.
6. Bassett, "Aeronautics on Long Island," p. 411.

Wings Over the Hempstead Plains, pages 15–22

1. C.R. Roseberry, *Glenn Curtiss: Pioneer of Flight* (Garden City, NY: Doubleday & Co., 1972), p. 175.
2. Henry Walden, "I Built and Flew America's First Monoplane," *Flying* (January 1958): 34.
3. Edward Peck, "The Aero Club of Long Island," *American Aviation Historical Society* 21 (Fall 1976): 269.
4. "Tribute To a Pioneer," *Model Airplane News*, June 1960, p.12.
5. Henry Villard, "Fabulous Belmont Park," *American Aviation Historical Society* 29 (Spring 1984): 20.
6. Julie Klym, "America's First Flight Academy," *AOPA Pilot* (October 1979): 67.
7. Tom Couch, *Bleriot XI*, National Air & Space Museum (Washington, DC: Smithsonian Institution Press, 1982), p. 66.
8. See E.P. Stein, *The Flight of the Vin Fiz* (New York: Arbor House, 1985).
9. See Adelaide Ovington, *An Aviator's Wife*, (New York: Dodd, Mead, 1920).

World War I—War in the Sky, pages 23–28

1. See Robert Casari, *U.S. Military Aircraft 1908 to 1917* (Privately printed, 1974).

2. Joshua Stoff, "Long Island: Cradle of Aviation Medicine," *Long Island Forum*, 45 (November 1982): 212.

3. Paul Jason, "The First Yale Unit," *Naval Aviation in World War I*, ed. Adrian Van Wyen, Chief of Naval Operations (Washington, DC: U.S. Navy, 1969), p. 21.

4. "The Curtiss Aeroplane and Motor Company," *Aircraft Yearbook 1919* (New York: Manufacturers Aircraft Association, 1919), p. 97.

5. H.F. Smith, "The World's First Cruise Missiles," *Air Force Magazine*, (October 1977): 43.

The "Golden Age" of Flight, pages 29–48

1. See Richard Smith, *First Across* (Annapolis, MD: Naval Institute Press, 1973).

2. See Patrick Abbott, *Airship* (New York: Scribner's, 1973).

3. "The First International Air Race," *Aviation*, (September 1919): 22.

4. See Louis Casey, *The First Nonstop Coast-to-Coast Flight and the Historic T-2 Airplane* (Washington, DC: Smithsonian Institution, 1964).

5. See Charles Lindbergh, *The Spirit of St. Louis* (New York: Scribner's, 1953).

6. See Elinor Smith, *Aviatrix* (New York: Harcourt Brace, 1981).

7. Edgar Bergman, "They Called It the Peel Glider Boat," *Air Progress*, Summer 1968, p. 79.

8. See Joshua Stoff and William Camp, *Roosevelt Field: World's Premier Airport* (Terre Haute, IN: Historic Aviation, 1989).

9. Joanne Lynn, "Women's Cradle of Aviation: Curtiss Field, Valley Stream," in *Evoking a Sense of Place*, ed. Joann P. Krieg (Interlaken, NY: Heart of the Lakes, 1988), p. 85.

10. See Richard Hallion, *Legacy of Flight* (Seattle: University of Washington Press, 1977).

11. See William Davenport, *Gyro* (New York: Scribner's, 1978).

12. "The LWF Engineering Company," *Aircraft Yearbook 1919* (New York: Manufactures Aircraft Association, 1919), p. 169.

13. Jerome Chandler, "Resurrecting the Burnelli Wing," *First Class* 2 (1983): 16.

14. See "Curtiss," *Aircraft Yearbook 1919*.

15. See Gerald Moran, *Aeroplanes Vought*, (Temple City, CA: Historical Aviation Album, 1978).

16. See Igor Sikorsky, *The Story of the Winged-S* (New York: Dodd, Mead, 1939).

17. See *Yesterday, Today, Tomorrow—Fifty Years of Fairchild Aviation* (Hagarstown, MD: Fairchild Hiller, 1970).

18. Robert Abernathy, "College Point's Early Aircraft Makers," *Long Island Forum*, 50 (January 1987): 15.

19. B. Denton, "The Privateer Amphibian," *Aviation Engineering* (February 1931): 33.

20. James Gilbert, "The Bird from Brooklyn," *Flying* (April 1970): 48.

21. Peter Bowers, "The Marchetti," *AOPA Pilot* (January 1967): 51.

22. Jim Mass, "Fall from Grace—The Brewster Aeronautical Corporation," *American Aviation Historical Society* (Summer 1985): 118.

World War II—Long Island: Arsenal of Freedom, pages 49–58

1. See Joshua Stoff, *The Thunder Factory: The History of the Republic Aviation Corporation*, (Poole, Dorset, England: Arms and Armour Press, forthcoming, 1990).

2. See Richard Thruelsen, *The Grumman Story* (New York: Praeger, 1976).

The Postwar Era: The Jet Age, pages 59–71

1. David Kaplan, "The Convertawings Quadrotor," *Newsletter of the American Helicopter Society* (August 1956): 3.

2. See Stoff, *The Thunder Factory*.

3. *See Michael Hardy, Sea, Sky and Stars* (Poole, Dorset, England: Arms and Armour Press, 1987).

Probing the Final Frontier, pages 75–94

1. Milton Lehman, *This High Man* (New York: Farrar, Straus, 1963), p. 240.

2. Peter Cooksley, *Flying Bomb* (New York: Scribner's, 1979), p. 141.

3. *Project Rigel* (Bethpage, New York: Grumman Aircraft Engineering Corp, 1952).

4. *This New Ocean, NASA History of Project Mercury* (Washington, DC: U.S. Government Printing Office, 1966), p. 137.

5. Thruelsen, *The Grumman Story*, p. 326.

6. See Stoff, *The Thunder Factory.*

7. See Joshua Stoff and Charles R. Pellegrino, *Chariots For Apollo: The Making of the Lunar Module* (New York: Atheneum, 1985).

8. See Neil Armstrong, *First on the Moon* (Boston: Little, Brown, 1970).

9. Stoff, *Chariots for Apollo,* p. 193.

10. Kevin Finneran, "Raising Construction to New Heights," *High Technology* (October 1986): 22.

Appendix: Aviation Manufacturers, pages 95–99

1. Peter Bowers, "The Marchetti," *AOPA Pilot* (January 1967): 51.

2. Jim Maas, "Fall from Grace—The Brewster Aeronautical Corporation," *American Aviation Historical Society, 30* (Summer 1985): 118.

3. James Gilbert, "The Bird from Brooklyn," *Flying* (April 1970): 48.

4. Jerome Chandler, "Resurrecting the Burnelli Wing," *First Class* 2 (1983): 16.

5. See "The Curtiss Aeroplane and Motor Company," *Aircraft Yearbook 1919* (New York: Manufacturers Aircraft Association, 1919).

6. Robert Abernathy, "College Point's Early Aircraft Makers," *Long Island Forum,* 50 (January 1987): 15.

7. See *Yesterday, Today, Tomorrow—Fifty Years of Fairchild Aviation* (Hagarstown, MD: Fairchild Hiller, 1970).

8. B. Denton, "The Privateer Amphibian," *Aviation Engineering* (February 1931): 33.

9. "The LWF Engineering Company," *Aircraft Yearbook 1919,* p.169.

10. See Igor Sikorsky, *The Story of the Winged-S* (New York: Dodd, Mead, 1939).

11. See William Davenport, *Gyro* (New York: Scribner's, 1978).

12. See Garard Moran, *Aeroplanes Vought* (Temple City, CA: Historical Aviation Album, 1978).

Bibliography

For further reading on various aspects of Long Island Aviation and Spaceflight.

Abbott, Patrick. *Airship, The Story of the R-34*. New York: Scribner's, 1973.

Allen, Peter. *The 91 Before Lindbergh*. Minneapolis, MN: Flying Books, 1985.

Anderton, David. *Republic F-105 Thunderchief*. London: Osprey, 1983.

Armstrong, Neil. *First on the Moon*. Boston: Little, Brown, 1970.

Bassett, Preston. "Aviation on Long Island." *Long Island: A History*, ed. Paul Bailey, II: 409–437. New York: Lewis Historical Publishing, 1949.

Berger, Carl. *The United States Air Force in Southeast Asia*. Washington, DC: Office of Air Force History, 1977.

Bilstein, Roger. *Flight in America 1900–1983*. Baltimore: Johns Hopkins, 1986.

Bowers, Peter. *Curtiss Aircraft 1907–1947*. Annapolis: Naval Institute Press, 1987.

Casari, Robert. *U.S. Military Aircraft 1908 to 1917*, Vol. 4. Privately printed: n. p., 1974.

Corn, Joseph. *The Winged Gospel*. New York: Oxford University Press, 1983.

Crouch, Tom. *A Dream of Wings: Americans and the Airplane, 1875 to 1905*. New York: W.W. Norton, 1981.

Davenport, William. *Gyro: The Life and Times of Lawrence Sperry*. New York: Scribner's, 1978.

Freeman, Roger. *Thunderbolt, A History of the Republic P-47*. New York: Scribner's, 1979.

Gill, Brendan. *Lindbergh Alone*. New York: Harcourt Brace, 1977.

Gunston, Bill. *One of A Kind: The Story of Grumman*. New York: Grumman, 1988.

Hallion, Richard. *Legacy of Flight: The Guggenheim Contribution to American Aviation.* Seattle: University of Washington Press, 1977.

Hardy, Michael. *Sea, Sky and Stars: An Illustrated History of Grumman Aircraft.* Poole, Dorset, England: Arms and Armour Press, 1987.

Husting, E.E. "Augustus Herring, Pioneer Aviator." *National Soaring Museum Journal* 1 (Winter 1976): 2–4.

Kaiser, William K., ed. *The Development of the Aerospace Industry on Long Island, 1904–1964.* Hofstra University, Yearbook of Business, 3 vols. Hempstead, NY: Hofstra University, 1968.

Lehman, Milton. *This High Man: The Life of Robert Goddard.* New York: Farrar, Straus, 1963.

Lindbergh, Charles. *The Spirit of St. Louis.* New York: Scribner's, 1953.

Maas, Jim. "Fall From Grace (Brewster Aeronautical Corporation 1932 to 1942)." *American Aviation Historical Society* 30 (Summer 1985): 118–32.

Maloney, Edward. *Sever The Sky: The Evolution of Seversky Aircraft.* Corona Del Mar, CA: Planes of Fame Publishers, 1979.

Oakes, Claudia. *United States Women in Aviation Through World War One.* Washington, DC: Smithsonian Press, 1985.

Peck, Edward. "The Aero Club of Long Island." *American Aviation Historical Society* 21 (Fall 1976): 269–74.

Roseberry, C.R. *Glenn Curtiss: Pioneer of Flight.* Garden City, NY: Doubleday, 1972.

———. *The Challenging Skies: Aviation 1919 to 1939.* Garden City, NY: Doubleday, 1966.

Simonson, G.R. *The History of the American Aircraft Industry.* Cambridge, MA: MIT Press, 1968.

Smith, Elinor. *Aviatrix.* New York: Harcourt Brace, 1981.

Smith, Richard. *First Across: The U.S. Navy's Transatlantic Flight of 1919.* Annapolis: Naval Institute Press, 1973.

Smits, Edward. *Nassau, Suburbia U.S.A.* Garden City, NY: Doubleday, 1974.

Stein, E.P. *The Flight of the Vin Fiz.* New York: Arbor House, 1985.

Stoff, Joshua. "America's First Powered Flights—Over Brooklyn!" *Long Island Forum* 48 (May 1985): 84–88.

_____. "The Brewster Buffalo: America's Worst Fighter?" *Air Combat*, Tokyo, 7 (Summer 1989): 14–23.

_____. "Grumman vs. Republic." *Long Island Historical Journal* 1 (Spring 1989): 113–125.

_____. "Long Island: Cradle of Aviation Medicine." *Long Island Forum* 45 (November 1982): 212–17.

_____. *The Thunder Factory: The History of the Republic Aviation Corporation.* Poole, Dorset, England: Arms & Armor Press, 1990.

Stoff, Joshua, and William Camp. *Roosevelt Field: World's Premier Airport.* Terre Haute, IN: Historic Aviation, 1989.

Stoff, Joshua, and Charles Pellegrino. *Chariots for Apollo: The Making of the Lunar Module.* New York: Atheneum, 1985.

Thruelsen, Richard. *The Grumman Story.* New York: Praeger, 1976.

Villard, Henry. *Contact: The Story of the Early Birds.* New York: Bonanza, 1968.

_____. "Fabulous Belmont Park." *American Aviation Historical Society* 29 (Spring 1984): 20–25.

Wiggin, Charles. *The First Transcontinental Flight.* New York: Bookmailer, 1961.

Index

Numbers in *italics* refer to illustrations. Plane models are listed by their name or number with manufacturer's name in parenthesis.

The Long Island Studies Institute

The Long Island Studies Institute at Hofstra University promotes and encourages the study of Long Island's history and heritage through its collections, conferences, programs, publications, educational resources, and services. The Institute was established in 1985, when the Nassau County Museum Reference Library moved to Hofstra, combining with Hofstra's New York State History collection to create a major resource for the study of Long Island local and regional history. The Institute, on the ninth floor of the Axinn Library, also houses the historical research offices of the Nassau County Historian and Division of Museum Services.

Publications

The Long Island Studies Institute serves Long Island and the broader historical community by sponsoring symposia, conferences, and publications to enhance awareness of Long Island's rich heritage. The 1986 Conference on Long Island Studies resulted in two publications edited by Joann P. Krieg: *To Know the Place: Teaching Local History* (1987) and *Evoking a Sense of Place* (1988). "Suburbia Re-Examined," the Institute's 1987 conference commemorating the 40th anniversary of Levittown, has two publications forthcoming in 1990, edited by Barbara M. Kelly: *Suburbia Re-Examined* and *Long Island: The Suburban Experience.* The Institute commemorated the Centennial of Robert Moses in 1988; the conference volume edited by Dr. Krieg is *Robert Moses: Single-Minded Genius* (1989). Selected papers from the Institute's 1989 conference, "Building Long Island: Architecture and Design; Tools and Trades," and the April 1990 conference, "Theodore Roosevelt and the Birth of Modern America" will be published.

Other publications of the Long Island Studies Institute

116

currently available include: *Long Island and Literature* (1989) by Joann P. Krieg and *Cumulative Index, Nassau County Historical Society Journal, 1958–1988,* compiled by Jeanne M. Burke (1989). For information on conferences and publications, contact the Long Island Studies Institue, Hofstra University, Hempstead, NY 11550, 516–560–5092.

Typeset on an Itek Digitek 3000 photocompositor in 11½ point Palatino® Medium on a 12½ baseline with heads in Italic and Semibold Italic.

Printed on 60 pound white and perfect bound in 8 point coated-one-side cover.

Contact Walt Steesy for your book publishing needs.

A *quality* publication from
Heart of the Lakes Publishing
Interlaken, New York 14847